Souled Out

ATTAIN YOUR NEXT-LEVEL LIFE DESPITE
UNEXPECTED OUTCOMES

Amy Westbrook

Camille Publishing

Souled Out / Amy Westbrook —1st ed.
ISBN 978-1-7353438-0-8 (pbk)
ISBN 978-1-7353438-1-5 (eBook)

Contents

Dedicated with love and gratitude...

To Jesus! I owe it all to you. Every trial, every stumble, every victory, every recalibration of my life—you have been and remain my driving force and saving grace. All of my roads have led back to you.

To Mother, I dedicate this book to you. You taught me to love deeply, and to thrive in the face of adversity. You taught me how to make life beautiful despite unexpected outcomes. All that you tirelessly, selflessly poured into me I desire to pour into the lives that God places in front of me.

To Lauren, I dedicate these words to you in hopes that you will continue to let them be a guide toward living a life of conquering the unconquerable and knowing that, alongside Christ, you have in you all that you need to achieve your dreams.

DISCLAIMER FROM THE AUTHOR

I am certainly aware that there are individuals who will not walk out of their wheelchair. It has been my honor to meet a handful of such individuals. Many of these amazing individuals have figured out how to live their next-level life far more wholly than have those of us with full mobility. The processes and truths in this book apply both to those who have use of their extremities as well as those who do not. Maximum mobility is an inside job, and it is available to all human beings. I continue to stand in awe of those who are bound to wheelchairs but are next-level lifers anyway!

GENERAL DISCLAIMER

The author of this book is not a physician. The ideas, suggestions, and advice provided are not intended as a substitute for the medical advice of a trained health professional and should only be used as a supplement to your doctor's advice. All matters regarding your health require medical supervision. The author and publisher disclaim any liability arising directly or indirectly from the use of this book.

SETTING THE STAGE

As a wife, mom, business owner, athlete, entrepreneur, and proverbial energizer bunny, I found myself in the ICU at Seton Hospital in Austin, Texas, having just had a tumor removed from inside my spinal cord. Residing between my shoulder blades at T4, it took five and a half hours to determine what was cord and what was tumor to remove. The surgeon had to get every cell in order to diminish the chances of it growing back. He said it looked like a grenade had gone off inside my spinal cord. Timing was everything. The integrity of the edge of the cord where the damage occurred was the thickness of a piece of paper. Had the tumor pressed through that space, I would have had no chance of recovery. I would have permanently had what is medically referred to as a complete spinal cord injury (CSI) as opposed to an incomplete spinal cord injury (ISI). There is no option for reversing the damage of a CSI, and the results are permanent paraplegia.

Have you ever found yourself in a situation that paralyzed you? There are so many situations in life that slam our mind, will, and emotions into lock down, including divorce, financial ruin, a broken home, unstable caregivers, and the loss of a job or expected promotion. The list of experiences that can be paralyzing is long: abuse, a sick child, and mental illness for starters. Even as I type these words, we are all suffering at some level from the Covid-19 disruptor. Millions are paralyzed with fear and uncertainty about the basic life needs from this unexpected pandemic. We are paralyzed by situations and events that happened yesterday or today, and we may be paralyzed by events that will happen in the future. Do you feel stuck? Are you sick and tired of being sick and tired?

I've been there, countless times. As a teenager I was paralyzed by disapproval of my appearance, lost in anorexic behavior. I was paralyzed by the shame that comes from using drugs and alcohol and the life it breeds. I was emotionally paralyzed by the effects of a boyfriend who shot himself because I broke up with him. I was spiritually paralyzed by a devastating church hurt.

I've been physically and emotionally abused, and that kind of abuse is paralyzing to your self-worth and your relationship patterns. Then, losing my mother—my hero, my rock—sixteen years ago emotionally stifled me. Adultery is paralyzing to a marriage. All of these I have lived through. Multiple episodes of betrayal and deceit place our survival systems in lockdown.

What paralyzed your past does not have to paralyze your future. I know this full well because my ultimate paralysis was physical. I was paraplegic.

This book is about getting you unstuck and mobile in the areas of your life where you are suffering and have lost hope. This book is for all of you who are wondering, *Will I make it out of this? Can I do this? Does God see my despair and pain? Will my dreams come true? I thought I would be more, do more, and have more by now? What is wrong with me? How do I tear down this roadblock? Hell, what is the roadblock? Is this all there is? Is this what my life is going to amount to? I have had success, but I haven't yet achieved my dreams.*

Friend, I cannot write fast enough as I picture your face asking me any (or all) of those questions. There are answers, solutions, and rescues on the way. This book will serve as a resource for the rest of your life as you ebb and flow through life, attaining varying degrees of your next-level experience. Through real life stories, universal truths, and taught processes it will also serve anyone who finds themselves smack dab in the middle of life.

Throughout the pages of this book I will share the unexpected outcome that changed my own life: physical paralysis. I will also share many other stories to serve as a rescue from what you find yourself going through right now. My book is for you if you are looking to overcome, if you need to know how to persevere because you aren't sure you have another hour left within you. If this is you, you've just found hope! Many people are in the midst of difficult transition, and I have the recipe to win through transition. My gift to you is to show you, prove to you, and encourage you that paralysis, lock down, or stuck-ness is not your last call. I help people "walk" again and find their next-level life. If I were still in sales and marketing, the commodity I would be selling is freedom. Freedom to live a life unencumbered in order to attain the "more" that you always dreamed was out there somewhere, waiting for you!

I am obsessed with freedom. Lock down is the opposite of freedom. Whether you are experiencing mental, emotional, or physical lock down, I know the way out. I am willing to give you a decade of answers in a single day.

We have all experienced pain, and that pain is a catalyst for us to evolve. In this moment, I want to meet you in the pain, frustration, and anger you may be in or may have experienced. I am truly sorry for your pain. Your story is so valuable, and it is far from over.

I recently got a text from a precious friend alerting me that her husband was diagnosed with a secondary cancer, meaning that there was a root location still to be identified. Ten days later, I am returning to this paragraph before the manuscript goes to the editor to include that he has passed away. Days after my friend's text, I received news that an acquaintance of mine and my daughter fell down her stairs and passed away. A mother in her forties with a daughter who is the same age as my daughter. In a nanosecond, I am reminded of how our entire being takes on devastating news or phone calls that put us on the ground. Please experience the comfort I am extending to you right there where you feel stuck, possibly in despair or extreme loneliness. Know that God will never leave you or forsake you, regardless of how you feel. I challenge you right now to get quiet and ask God what He has to say about your point of paralysis. Yes, you can access the spirit of God. What does He want you to know? Ask Him if He knows how you feel? Just sit and listen, and let the God of ALL comfort begin to surround you and move you towards maximum mobility. He will show up on your behalf.

When I was in the hospital after my spinal cord surgery, one of my dearest friends brought a journal to me and had inscribed this passage inside of it: "You're not the only ones plunged into these hard times. It's the same with Christians all over the world. So keep a firm grip on the faith. The suffering won't last forever. *It won't be long before this generous God who has great plans for us in Christ—eternal and glorious plans they are!—will have you put together and on your feet for good. He gets the last word; yes, He does…* The Message translation of the Bible says this in 1 Peter 5:10-11.

For those of you who simply can't stand another trip around the same mountain and are ready for a freedom that will catapult you to your next level life, I've got you! Just ahead is the guide to the mental fortitude you are needing to scale the next wall. You will also learn the critical skill of maintaining the mind-body connection.

The insight, miracles, and wisdom from this book will put hope back in your heart and the belief that you too can *walk out of the "wheelchair" life has placed you in*.

In these seasons of lockdown, I have learned that the way we choose to respond versus react, who we choose to forgive (or not), and what we are willing to receive out of a situation all determine if we will ever truly walk again in those areas of our lives affected by paralysis.

As I discovered through physical paralysis, when one area is paralyzed, the sum of the parts begins to break down as well. You cannot be paralyzed in one area of your life and have nothing else affected. It is impossible. That is why we can have unresolved, paralyzing childhood experiences that cause us to struggle in our professions as adults. Multiple distractions begin to occur during the state of paraplegia, and you find yourself not only battling against being crippled but also battling for every system tied to the root. Does any of this sound familiar? Does any of this resonate with where you are or where you have been? These types of paralysis and the symptoms that follow are common. You are not alone. There is nothing wrong with you. You just haven't discovered the *how* of it until today. Behind every closed door, behind every beautiful smile, we all have battled, will battle, or are battling some form of the P word.

Not one of us is immune to "unexpected outcomes." The title Queen of Unexpected Outcomes has attached itself to me. It's not one I chose; it chose me. With everything inside of me, I will use my life stories to guide you out of your state of paralysis or your unexpected outcome with maximum mobility, decisiveness, and clarity. You will have the opportunity to reset your mind to the truth. The truth being, you *can* bring life and mobility to areas of your life that have been in lockdown for far too long.

It's not over for you. Your life is not stalled out until they close the casket (and honestly, that is when true living really begins!). You are more than what the mound of mess facing you amounts to. You have not used up all of your passes to the entrance of the life you've always wanted.

Let me pause here and mention that we can be in a heightened state of movement and still be paralyzed. Just because your body and mind are experiencing rapid movement doesn't mean your problem to solve is not paralysis. In fact, chaos often breeds paralysis of our mind, will, and emotions. It literally shuts them down. So does the trauma found within unexpected outcomes. Our brains are designed to always be on the lookout for danger and for the way to keep us safe – to survive. I'm a bit of a brain science fanatic, and throughout this book I will deposit insights every person should know about our fascinating brains' abilities. It is a top priority of interest if you desire an exceptional life.

I cannot impress you with movie star credentials or tell you I have been to heaven and back. What I can do is relate to you and help you get out of lockdown in order to live your next-level life. I have not spent a lot of time on social media building thousands of "likes." My time has instead been spent developing methods to overcome unexpected outcomes, methods that I am now ready to share with others. You will find next-level life answers and processes throughout every chapter. In regard to healing, you will find my heart and compassion poured into the pages of this book, and that will bring you to your revelation. In writing this book, I made an all-out effort to save you a massive amount of time and money by cutting to the chase. I have delivered within the pages ahead the process of how to get out of the spin cycle.

This book is a download of over three decades of trial and error, thriving out of the trenches, and growth from real-life experiences. You will see that my journey out of physical paralysis is so very relatable to this journey called life. And lastly, for many of you this journey will shake the foundations of what you potentially believe about a God who speaks directly to the details of our lives.

Entering spinal cord surgery, I was coming off a six-year misdiagnosis. I had withstood multiple MRIs, a half dozen surgeons, visits to MD Anderson in Houston and to Johns Hopkins Medical Center in Baltimore. The diagnosis was repeatedly missed. It wasn't until we went to the surgical table that we would find the truth. Not a cavernous angioma (a bundle of blood vessels malformed) but a tumor that had ruptured out and caused a total mess inside my control tower. Things were not as we expected them to be.

Isn't life like that? It doesn't turn out as we plan, as we envision, or as we diagnose. This is a book about *overcoming the unexpected outcomes* that cause paralysis. Outcomes that seem to alter our life forever and either shatter us or better us. It truly is dependent upon our response. I realize that you may not feel like you have much control over your response or the outcome in the midst of the paralysis. The key is this: you cannot change the unexpected outcome or the storm it has already manifested. *You can, however, change how it affects the remainder of your life, the condition of your heart, and the mental well-being you emerge with.*

During a time in my life when I was emotionally paralyzed from domestic abuse, a woman spoke a similar sentence to me. She had shared a rather lengthy poem with the overall theme that I had a choice in how I responded. It didn't have to be with despair. I thought she was totally clueless. Clueless about the severity of the situation, clueless about the depth of my fear and anxiety. Looking back, I realize she was trying to *inspire my power back to me.* I ultimately had the power to determine how much the trauma would take from me and how much havoc I *allowed* it to own in my life, both then and moving forward. She was trying to guide me to a *perspective change* and to the reality of choice. At that time, when I was twenty-six years old, I did not, I could not, grasp the concept that I could see the trauma any other way. There is a great deal about perspective change throughout my life story. A game changer occurs when we grow our ability to analyze perspective in order to gain maximum clarity as to what is really happening within paralysis. I call it becoming an observer. Through learning about my experience, you will begin to learn how to gain that perspective more and more quickly. *When achieved, it is a power position full of freedom.* I didn't always get it right, but the times I did are diabolically different from those when I didn't.

I wish I could tell you that I entered the hospital on a spiritual high, but I did not. I entered the hospital having just experienced, ironically, many months of spiritual paralysis. But God uses all things, and indeed He used the hospital to heal one of the deepest wounds I have ever known.

This is my story, His testimony. Over and over I have found rescue from paralysis. It wasn't until gaining back my physical mobility that I realized the principles of paraplegia were similar to principles I had been applying all my life to overcome other unexpected outcomes. It was from that epiphany that I began to develop a method for living life that I named The Freedom Success Method™ This success model is built around clarity, decisiveness, healing, and action.

Through ministry work I have helped hundreds of women walk out of far worse paralyzing circumstances than I have endured. They applied many of the principles coming your way to recover, and have walked in freedom, having been dead spirits and even broken souls unable to say "I love you" to their children. They have started businesses, launched products, repaired marriages, and forgiven themselves and those who immensely damaged them. If applied, you too can walk again in freedom. Although I have not walked in your specific shoes, I believe that the shoes I have walked in for the past three decades allow me to serve you into healing for more success.

I am a spiritual being, and that is the lens through which I see life. That is the lens through which I wrote this book. When I was a young girl, I became a Christian, but it was not until my thirtieth birthday that I truly committed to a Christ who became Lord of my life. The radical spiritual transformation I went through led me to create a 501c3 to help other women experience the same freedom journey that I had encountered. It was a freedom I could not, would not, keep to myself.

Thank you in advance for allowing me the freedom to be exactly who I am as I share my story and, in turn, my faith throughout this manuscript. The two cannot be separated.

The one other idea I want to introduce as we dive into this miraculous journey together is that I decided to shorten the projected length of my book for a couple of reasons. First, statistics say that only three percent of people finish a 200-plus page book, and I want you to finish so that the entire message can change your life. Second, I want to teach my book. Although I can help you create and advance your momentum through the stories contained in this book, an online course can advance you exponentially. It provides a way for you to apply the truths and processes to your personal life with outcomes of healing, restoration, and advancement.

The Freedom Success Method™ delivers small chunks of teachings instead of a 200-plus-page book you would possibly never finish. I want you to succeed and be moved to take action. I can download three decades of experience into a course more effectively than I can into an excessively lengthy book. My online course provides even more of a "how to" and "hands on" approach to achieving your next-level life. It brings mobility to dead spaces. If you are simply wanting to grow and get closer to your dreamed-about destiny in life or in business, The Freedom Success Method™ more than accomplishes that goal.

THE TUMOR

et's travel backward to four years prior to my surgery, when the tumor was first revealed. It was a regular day during a great time in my life. That day, little did I know, was setting me up for the rest of my life. I was married to the love of my life, and we owned our first home. I was really happy. We spent time on Lake Austin, wakeboarding and enjoying a crazy, healthy lifestyle.

A few years prior I left my position as Director of Business Development for a five-station radio group. I was born with an entrepreneurial gene, so I headed out the radio door to run my own marketing and business development company, The !dea House. Greg (my husband at the time) and I also ran an international trade show that I bought just before leaving the radio group. I was in my fourth year serving on the board of the Candlelighters Childhood Cancer Foundation. Greg and I spent a lot of time in the gym together. I spent a lot of time running at Lady Bird Lake and roller blading in our neighborhood.

The biggest thing I had going in my life was a radical spiritual renewal. My life, from birth to my thirtieth birthday, was filled with a lot of brokenness. Much of it was brought on by my own behavior, and much of it was brought on by outside sources. All the places I had been roadblocked, stuck, and even paralyzed God was now clearing out in order to set me free. I read twenty-six books that year, including the Bible, in a search and rescue effort for my soul. Don't get me wrong, I was a high-functioning individual, but internally I was in lockdown. The only pain the spirit of God hadn't gotten hold of yet was debilitating neck pain from an injury I acquired at birth. This condition had caused chronic pain since I was in grade school.

I was at my breaking point with the pain and had seen a neurologist about treatment. That is the day we got the news for the first time. We had a normal conversation about the MRI for my neck pain and mapped out a plan. The minute she closed her file, she said, "Can you guys please step out here in the hallway? I have something else I want you to see." There, posted on an X-ray screen, was another image of my MRI. This image, however, had my spinal cord lit up light a Christmas tree. She was vague and short in her explanation, but what was clear was the mass inside my spinal cord. She told us that the technician found it as he scanned my neck. We were referred to a neurosurgeon, and that was that.

Weeks later we found ourselves at MD Anderson in the neurosurgery department with three doctors in the room. After much deliberation, several things were determined. One, the mass cocooned inside my spinal cord was diagnosed as a cavernous angioma, a malformation of blood cells similar to a nest or web. They can hemorrhage and paralyze, or they can lay dormant forever.

Two, my cavernous angioma was seemingly lying dormant, because I had absolutely no detectable symptoms. Nonetheless, it presented as having been there for a long time and with substantial hemorrhage.

Three, no one was going to do anything about it.

The possibility of me going through life without a problem was high. And, as high-functioning as I was at examination, no one was going to touch my spinal cord.

The MD Anderson team strongly advised not birthing a baby or lifting exceptionally heavy weights-both activities that could cause a sudden rise in blood pressure or rapid increase in blood flow, hemorrhaging the mass in the cord and causing certain paralysis. (Interestingly, I had previously smoked for years and had been an avid weightlifter up until that day.) Just a few months prior to this discovery, I had a miscarriage. Not knowing about the mass at the time, in superior physical condition, I certainly would have birthed that baby. At that point I felt incredibly protected!

I called my mom the minute we got in the car and shared the good news. We traveled back to Austin, and in absolute faith we moved on and laid the issue aside.

Fast forward sixteen months. My life was full and rich doing things I loved to do. I was director of a Chamber of Commerce women's business group, was leading a freedom ministry for our vastly growing church, and was running The !dea House. Greg and I were immersed in our church and were at an all-time spiritual high. As a hobby, I taught three aerobics classes a week at the church and also taught healthy living classes in our home. I finally became pregnant, scheduled the C-section as recommended by the MD Anderson surgeons, and a five-pound four-ounce baby girl was gifted to me. My life had not been so good in a really long time.

I have often heard that the very worst in life happens simultaneously with the most glorious. That is exactly what happened for me. We had tried for this baby girl for almost two years. She finally arrived just before my mother, who was my rock, would abruptly die from a rare form of Leukemia. How could this be? Finally, my life was all straightened out. I had big plans to make up for lost time from all those broken years when I let my shallow, self-indulged life shut out our time together. And now, my child was going to be cheated out of knowing my female hero, and the woman I most desired to emulate was about to be gone forever. Never mind the fact that I needed her guidance as a new mother. After all, she was put on this earth to be a mother.

She passed when my daughter Lauren was just four months old. The devastation left in my siblings and me was paramount. Everyone pulled it together and we made life happen for ourselves and for her eight grandchildren, who would have to know her through the ways we lived and loved.

A few years passed, and yet another catastrophic wave of pain hit. Greg and I experienced a church-related hurt that completely took us to our knees.

While it isn't necessary to go into the intimate details of the hurt, I recognize that many others have also experienced deep and everlasting wounds from an experience at church—one of the last places we believe we will experience such pain. I share my experience in brief only to let you know that I understand, and that I know that restoration can come to your soul and spirit.

My experience involved being discarded from a volunteer ministry leadership position that I had invested in at a deep level. Overnight, I felt abandoned by a couple hundred people I had loved, poured into, and done life with. Church-related hurts can be incredibly damaging because the infraction messes with the deepest part of who we are as humans.

The bottom line is, people both intentionally and unintentionally fail other people. The Bible states that the author of confusion and dissension is the devil himself. Do not play into his hand. He is perfectly intending to disqualify your spiritual existence with a huge infraction in your soul. That infraction then attaches to your personal and professional life as a root of bitterness and resentment. With your spirit shut down, you will never be whole

***

Given that Greg had been a custom home builder for over fifteen years, we eventually sold the trade show and started a custom home building company. As co-owner, I earned my real estate license and helped with marketing and investor relations.

2007 was a brand-new year, and our daughter was three. Our newly formed company, Dillon Custom Homes, had only been in operation for a few years, so money was really tight. As if there hadn't been enough unexpected outcomes already, the bottom was about to fall out of our lives. My health had been deteriorating at an alarming rate. The physical symptoms dramatically ramped up that January starting with severe lower back pain. I finally went for an MRI in August when a pins and needles sensation set into my legs along with a lack of sensation in my feet. The thought honestly never entered my mind that there could be a problem with the mass between my shoulder blades. The pain was, after all, in my lower back. I simply assumed I had hurt my lower back in some way while running or exercising. As instructed, I had laid off the weightlifting for some time but had continued to teach three aerobics classes per week up until the day Lauren was born, and I continued to run and do Pilates.

The pain had not only become brutal in my lower back, it had become physically and mentally exhausting. By late afternoon, I began to run out of steam and the nightly regimen became repetitive. I would sit in the rocker and allow Greg and Lauren to wait on me hand and foot. This had been going on for months!

Greg and I arrived at Dr. White's office, the recommended neurologist who had ordered the MRI. He greeted us somberly, and I was about to figure out why.

"The mass in your spinal cord is hemorrhaging substantially. I recommend you revisit the neurosurgeon who examined you at MD Anderson four years ago. You will have to travel to Baltimore though, he is now the Director of Neurosurgery for Johns Hopkins Medical Center." I was stunned. "You have got to be kidding me," I declared. A surge of emotions flew through my body. "I am just forty years old; this cannot be happening!"

I was breathless, taken aback by his comments. Four years prior, the neurosurgeons at MD Anderson made it all too clear to me the repercussions of this "thing" rearing its head, and the detail of that conversation came rushing in. I couldn't even process in that moment where Johns Hopkins Medical Center was.

Doctor Gokaslan was a perceived "guru" of the cavernous angioma that was supposedly inside my spinal cord. There had been absolutely zero symptoms four years prior, yet the extent of the symptoms I was now suffering with caused fear to grip my gut. This man surely was the answer. This guru of the rare and potentially lethal cavernoma. If I could just get to him, he would be my answer.

We had to scrape together the money needed to get to Baltimore. We spent the next day calling friends and family, borrowing frequent flyer points to get there. We touched down in Baltimore, rented a wheelchair, and were off to the appointment. No fewer than three surgeons as well as the director himself reviewed my films. After physical examination, much to my surprise, the conclusion was the same as it had been five years prior: do nothing! Except for excruciating lower back pain, I presented as a fit, overall healthy forty-year-old woman, and they did not want to mess that up. The potential for the surgery to damage my mobility was quite high. The surgery was far too risky to perform until they were more certain that it would not make me worse than I already was. In other words, if I had come in paralyzed and incontinent, they would have performed surgery. Both were likely outcomes of the surgery. At this point, I was guaranteed that with surgery I would never be the same. I was sent for a Band-Aid of injections to block the pain.

The injections proved useless, so we returned to Baltimore a second time. Again, no surgery was recommended. The risks still far outweighed the benefits of cutting into my cord. There was a higher than comfortable morbidity rate and only a five percent chance that I would not become paralyzed.

The travel from both trips was grueling on my back and greatly increased my pain. Greg had pushed me through the streets of Baltimore and along the waterfront as we waited for various doctor appointments. At one point, we were downtown looking for a recommended restaurant. Potentially lost, we were in a really rough part of Baltimore with many vagrants lining the streets. Greg went into a tiny corner liquor store for directions and parked me outside with a homeless man and another man in a wheelchair. Thanks, Greg! As I sat there, petrified, I consoled myself with the thought that surely even hardened criminals and drunks would not attack me, a woman in a wheelchair.

During this second visit, they conducted a nerve study, which was just to confirm whether my physical problems were coming from an old back issue or from the tumor. It was confirmed that the tumor was the initiating point, at T-4 (between my shoulder blades). Silently, I had been wishing they would discover that wear and tear on my back was the problem. The news left me numb inside, knowing that, eventually, something possibly catastrophic would have to be done to remedy the problem. Life as I knew it was about to change.

There in the lobby of the hospital, I sat and waited for Greg to pull the truck around. Tears streamed down my face. A lady stopped, touched my shoulder, and asked, "Are you okay?" I nodded my head, my mind frozen on what possibly lie ahead. And there it was, an all too familiar voice that had been so absent from my life the past year. As if it were yesterday, I can recall that moment with clarity. Sitting on that bench, the deep love of wisdom spoke into my despair. I heard, *"I will not abandon the works of my hand."* I got in the truck, gave Greg the results of the test, and told him what I had just heard. It wasn't a thundering voice but thoughts—and they were absolutely not my own. The thoughts were, *"I will not abandon the works of my hand."* This is the way God most often speaks to me, through thoughts, and I am beyond clear that they are higher wisdom.

This word is now for you as well. It came to me at a time of great fear, filled with many unknowns and what ifs. I declare this over your life today in this very moment. "He is faithful! He will not abandon the works of His hand." His work is *you*. Your despair or fear or anxiety or anger cannot drown Him out of your life. Unexpected outcomes do not mean that He is absent. He will get to you and pursue you with relentless effort.

The days passed on, the pain worsened, and my condition took a nosedive. After walking no more than forty feet on any given day, I was literally paralyzed by pain and could not take additional steps. With the decline that had ensued, we were encouraged to go back in for another MRI and scheduled a trip back to Johns Hopkins. We would never make it to that appointment. I became homebound, and fatigue restricted me from experiencing the basics of life. One day, as I stood in the grocery store, paralyzed, unable to move my feet, my sister came to rescue me. I was seriously in trouble and needed a miracle.

After approximately eighteen months, we reconciled with the church, ironically as the pastor was presenting a series on miracles. We received an apology and an explanation for all the misunderstandings involved. We were bathed in prayer and love. The featured scripture that particular Sunday was Psalm 118:17 (NIV): I will not die but live and will proclaim what the Lord has done. I saw clearly the timing of our return.

Now homebound, I knew I would have to find a neurosurgeon ASAP in Austin who would see me in this new state of crisis. Lying immobile on the couch one weekend, realizing I was not going to be able to get on the plane to attend the appointment we'd made at Johns Hopkins, I began to repetitively pray: "I trust you, God; I trust you, God; I trust you, God." It almost overtook me. I succumbed to my higher power, the Holy Spirit, the situation. Desperate, I continued to repeat "I trust you, God; I trust you."

The significance of that prayer was profound to my soul, having recently emerged from a spiritual betrayal that led to a lack of trust in whether or not God really had my back. My trust in God had been at an all-time low over the past twelve or so months. Of course, the truth is that people have free will, and God does not control us like robots. We get angry at an infallible God when a fallible man makes mistakes and inflicts pain.

As I prayed, there was a shift happening deep within me. My paralyzed heart was again starting to beat. Unable to return to Johns Hopkins, the question became, *What will I do? Who will take my case?* The guru at Johns Hopkins was the one who was supposed to help me, and I could not get to him. Where would my help come from? The maker of heaven and earth.

Alone, hurting, and scared, I began to pray again and again. The need for and reality of the level of faith and trust I would place in my higher power consumed me. I continued with the "I trust you Lord" prayer and enlarged it to include "Lord, give me the doctor with the mind and the hands here locally. God, supernaturally lead me to them." There in the quiet of our home I went to the computer and reviewed the two acclaimed brain and spine groups I knew of in Austin. I reviewed all their accomplishments, credentials, and degrees. I studied their faces and pleaded for God to show me who to choose. One man finally stood out: Dr. Craig Kemper. He accepted our urgent case and had us come in right away. Dr Kemper turned out to be one of the most acclaimed neurosurgeons in the city. "I trust you, Lord, I trust you." Those words would prepare me for what Dr. Kemper would say to us the next day.

The nurse wheeled me out to the restroom, and my husband asked the surgeon what his initial reaction was to what he saw on my films. Greg said, "I want your honest truth. What did you think?" Dr. Kemper replied, "Well, I said, 'Oh sh*t!'" His astonishment at the results of my MRI prompted a heated conversation. He indeed was what this type-A, tell-me-how-it-is girl needed. Candidly, he shared, "I don't want to scare you or offend you, but you are in serious trouble. You are becoming paralyzed inch by inch, day by day. If this 'thing' ruptures, you are out of luck. And that could happen at any moment. I have taken these out of brains, spinal cords, and eyeballs, and I can take it out of your spinal cord."

Yes! Finally, someone who would tell it to me straight. Doctor after doctor had backed up from doing anything for me in fear that the removal of the mass would paralyze me for life. Now, this doctor was confident that I would be up and moving day of surgery, as had his other patients. He expected me to gain back a lot, if not all, of the functionality I had already lost. Dr. Kemper concluded, "You have to make a decision, and soon. Come back in a week with your answer."

That next week included more of the same debilitating pain and restriction. We scheduled the surgery, and I was given a dose of steroids to tide me over until then. The plan was for a surgery that would take two or three hours followed by a two-day stay in the hospital. I never saw it coming—lying paraplegic in the ICU, that is.

There were exactly ten days between the day we first saw Dr. Kemper and the surgery. Those were very dark, scary days. Just me, just God. Lying on our sofa knowing what was approaching. Everyone was eager for the surgery because I was in such bad shape. They were all hoping for a solution to the extreme pain they had seen me suffer with for so long. I, on the other hand, was not so eager. I knew that the surgery was *the* chance to turn this thing around, but also that there was a chance I might not ever walk again. Regardless of the horrible shape I was in, I could at least walk a few steps to the bathroom, the kitchen, or the couch. My legs still did work a little bit. Would they ever again after surgery ten days later?

The fear, the trust, the battle was raging on the sofa, in my body, and in my emotions. Oh, how I needed my mom. I needed her to talk to, to hold my hand. Years earlier when the mass was first detected, she was with Greg and me during one of our hospital visits. I was fully aware the news had shattered her. She had seen her daughter struggle time and time again, and now this. She tried hard to be brave.

When she was nearing the end of her life, I recall sitting next to her bed for hours in the hospital while she shifted between conscious and unconscious, just holding her hand. What a comfort it was both to me and to her. Lying there on the sofa, I longed for that comfort. Lying there, flat on my back, crying while buried deep in my warm blanket, it un-monumentally happened. To this day, I have told very few people about what then occurred on that sofa.

As I write, I can, all these years later, feel the fabric of the sofa against my skin. I can feel how melded into that couch I was. Tears, sobs, crying out to God. I needed Mom. Greg and Lauren had left the house for church and lunch. In my despair, I almost unconsciously raised my left hand over my head to the top of the back of the couch for someone to hold my hand. I squeezed my fingers as tightly as I could. I felt a level of comfort, as if someone physically grasped my hand. A very real connection was made, just like skin on skin. After a few minutes, this very real presence moved to the front of the couch. I let go with my left hand, moved to my right, and clinched the connection in the same way. After a few minutes the intensity decreased, and

I gently let go, calmer and more comforted. I knew I was not alone. I sensed a heavy covering over me as I relaxed back, deep into the sofa.

What do I think happened that day? One of several things. In alignment with my faith, I know there are angels of the Lord that do His bidding, and the Holy Spirit is an ever-present help in time of need. He, the Holy Spirit, is our comforter. That day, I believe I experienced the manifestation of an angel of the Lord.

My family was prepared, and yet we were all very scared. The only way I can describe the day to come is, skydiving without a parachute. I told my friend, "I feel like I have a date scheduled to jump out of an airplane with no parachute. If God doesn't show up to catch me, I am facing mobility death. And yet, there isn't an option not to jump!" This overwhelming thought sent me to the floor on my knees, a place I hadn't been but for a handful of times in the previous few weeks and months due to the spiritual angst I'd been managing. I was one day away from surgery. I was desperate, hurting, and seeking His face. On my knees in prayer, the voice of God came. The voice was oh-so-familiar but had been absent as of late. *This moment was pivotal* because after having been in spiritual lockdown, taking this next step forward would swing the doors wide open for God to take over my wounded heart and spirit. The spirit of God is a gentleman. He will not barge in; He waits for us to knock willingly. It is there in the knocking that He will be found standing at the doorway of surrender and of partnership.

Never could I have known the depth of pain and rejection that can come from a church-related hurt. It makes perfect sense because the spirit and soul are at the depths of our being, and that is the part that absorbs the blow. Perceived abandonment in the midst of church leadership is crippling. In our lives,

God is the alpha and the omega the beginning and the end, but He is also the middle of those two bookends. We can clearly see an omnipotent God as the beginning and the end, but we fail to realize that he is also in the middle. The middle of our trauma, our confusion, our loss. God's promise is not that we won't find ourselves in the "middle," but that He will guide us through the "middle." Whatever your "middle" looks like today, He is present. He was there in the "middle" of the church upheaval orchestrating reconciliation, and He knew we would meet again there with me on my knees, one day out from surgery.

That day on the floor, I finally willingly opened the door. On my knees, I prayed about the day I was about to face head-on. The prayer was over, and as was customary, I paused and asked God what, if anything, He wanted to deposit into my heart. I had been journaling for about seven years at that point and had spent hundreds of hours training myself and trusting to recognize God's voice and prompts—prompts from His spirit that I know lives within me. In that pause, anticipating His wisdom, nothing came, so I rose from my knees. Halfway to standing, I heard, "This is my testimony." For a millisecond I thought, "Ha! Yes! This *is* my testimony alright!" But, it came again so strong that I was compelled to go back down on my knees. No, not my testimony, it is His. It is not my pain but His comfort. It is not my fear but His security. It is not my efforts but His victory. I've always known that Godly testimonies are full of miraculous intervention. There on my knees, a measure of hope was deposited.

That afternoon I called my long-time best friend, who also happened to be my running partner. I cried as I told her where we were with our decisions. She encouraged me, and that was that.

It was time to pack my bags.

Jeremiah 29:11 (NIV): "For I know the plans I have for you," declares the Lord, "plans to prosper you and not to harm you, plans to give you hope and a future. Then you will call on me and come and pray to me, and I will listen to you. You will seek me and find me when you seek me with all your heart. I will be found by you," declares the Lord."

THE FIRST 48 HOURS

My family and friends arrived well before breakfast to see me off to surgery. We were all expecting to see each other again in just a couple of short hours. Little did we know, the clock would strike 7:30pm before they were admitted to see me in the ICU.

Just prior to being taken to the operating room, our friends and family left the room and my husband and I stared at each other. "Can you believe this?" I asked him. Shaking his head, he replied with a simple, somber, "No." A million things must have been racing through Greg's mind at that moment. The "what ifs" and most certainly the $10,000 deductible staring him in the face (in addition to whatever expenses would not be covered by our self-employment insurance). We prayed, and then the surgical team entered the room and began preparation.

Two girls on the OR team who were about my age popped in to say they would be monitoring my sensory and mobility function during surgery to ensure that those functions stayed intact at all costs. As we locked eyes, I said, "I have a four-year-old at home, and I love to run. Please, please do a good job." My neurosurgeon, Dr. Kemper, arrived and said he was ready to go. The day passed; the clock ticked.

A friend of mine recapped what the surgeon said as he entered the private family waiting room after a grueling surgery, the details of which he did not anticipate. Here is a snapshot of what she wrote:

"The surgeon walked in and approached us. As he removed his cap and began to speak, he was obviously exhausted. His words were careful and guarded. His demeanor was very serious. As we all sat with nervous anticipation, he explained that what he had found embedded in your spinal cord was a large tumor. I remember seeing the emotion in your dad when he said that. My heart ached for him. Greg looked very serious and stricken. Upon explaining that it looked like a grenade had exploded in your spinal cord, he described the difficulty he had in knowing whether he had gotten all of the tumor. Much of his time had been spent meticulously determining what was cord and what was actually tumor that needed to be removed. The boundaries were incredibly blurred, and he felt very uncertain in confirming that this nightmare was over. His honesty was painful as he told us that he had to make the decision to stop invading the cord when the nurses announced that you had lost sensory function. One millimeter too far and they would announce loss of motor function. You would be paralyzed permanently.

"I remember asking the doctor what the consequences of the sensory damage would be. He replied that you would have little feeling in your feet and would experience the sensations of having your feet falling asleep most of the time. Finding your balance would be your greatest challenge. As we listened, we all realized the seriousness of what he was saying. When asked if you would walk, he told us that his goal was simply for you to be happy one year from now. I thought that was such a strange thing for him to say, but in hindsight, I realize it was the most hope he could come up with. He told us that you would remain in inpatient rehab hospital through Christmas, and then he excused himself. For the first time through the long and grueling hours of that day, Greg buried his head in his hands and cried. We all cried. We cried for him, for you, and for Lauren."

When I woke up from surgery, the clock read 7:30pm. I must have looked like Lucille Ball after she had her last swig of Vegevegavitamin. Batting my eyes and licking my morphined-out lips, I thought, "Seven thirty? We started at eleven in the morning!" It never dawned on me that something had gone terribly wrong. My family and friends, who had waited literally all day outside the OR, were invited to come into my room in small groups to see me. My dad and Greg were first, then my precious friends and a representative from the church.

I don't remember much from the stupor I was in the first night of recovery, but the next morning I began to gab to anyone who would listen. As the ICU nurses scurried by my door I would talk and then fall back to sleep, talk some more and then fall back to sleep. Some replied from the hallway, and some said, "Wow, you sure are sounding great considering yesterday's ordeal." Trust me...how great I sounded was all drug related! We now know that I have a lot to say while under the influence of morphine (and I have a lot to say while *not* under the influence of morphine)!

What I remember clearly is the conversation I had with the surgeon when he came in to check on me. No one had informed me that the original plan was not carried out in that operating room. The diagnosis changed on the operating table, and so did the plan for recovery. The mass was not a cavernous angioma, as diagnosed at MD Anderson and Johns Hopkins Hospital.

My planned two-hour surgery and subsequent three days in the hospital turned out to be a five-and-a-half-hour surgery and two months in the hospital. The surgery took place the week after Thanksgiving, and I would stay in the hospital into the new year. At a time when everyone was festive and celebratory, I was lying in a cold bed in a cold room, listening to life flight land just outside my window, night after night. There, I grieved the loss of my mobility and the helplessness I felt, dependent on someone to come and roll me from side to side, diaper me, and bath me. Thank you, God, for those nurses, who were willing to work through the holidays to serve and care for me.

Plans change. Life disrupts really good plans. The surgeon began to examine me and talk with his assistant about the chances of me walking again. He looked at me and asked, "Do you know what is going on?" I furrowed my brow. "Well, what I found was not expected." He went on to explain that he found an ependymoma tumor, not a cavernous angioma. "We sent it off to see if it is benign. Results should be back Monday." He said he had to go way deeper into the cord than anticipated. He was pretty certain he got it all, but he said, "I had to stop to ensure I didn't hurt you any further. My eyes were saying stop and my mind was saying keep going." He was diligent in determining what was cord and what was tumor. It was imperative that he get all of the tumor or it would return. As he stood at the foot of my bed, I could tell by the look on his face he was hoping I would walk again. I was praying I would run again.

All my life, I've loved to run. I am a runner. I did not want to just walk; I wanted to run again. I had dreams of running with my daughter around Lady Bird Lake in downtown Austin, my jogging path for over fifteen years. All throughout my pregnancy I continued to run around that lake. As soon as Lauren was strong enough, I pushed her in her jogger around that lake. Eventually, she ran alongside the jogger as a toddler.

Days like that made my heart sing, and they were scrolling through my head. I can see that sunny day when she discovered how fun it was to jog alongside mommy. Lauren had been on that trail over a hundred times by that point, part of the time in my tummy and part of the time in the stroller. And then on her own. All along the winding path, or at least once we got past the duck and turtle pond, the squirming began with a fervent request: "Let me out, Mommy, Lauren run wit' you." On the home stretch, I would cave to her cuteness and release her from the apparatus that bound her. Off she would go—jogging and zig zagging from one side of the trail to another. The rule was that she had to hang on to the hand strap of the jogger, which kept her from running right down any ravines. Head looking one direction, legs going the other, we always managed to get to the finish line without incident. I had many plans for my life, and none of them included paralysis.

I am going to take a wild guess that your life plans did not involve paralysis either—paralysis of the body, heart, or mind. As I type these words twelve years after the unexpected outcome, tears well up in my eyes. Even though I walk free, there is something very emotional about the reality of the trauma, even after healing comes. My story involves the journey out of physical paralysis, but it also involves the journey out of other forms of paralysis. There is hope, because I am no longer frozen in any of these areas of my life. There is hope for you too.

There are a few defining truths about hope. Hope is not a feeling. Yet, the power of hope is real! It is a supportive life force and the wisdom hidden behind seeming chaos. If hope is seen within all unexpected outcomes, it opens the potential of the outcome exponentially!

Through the following steps, stories, and processes, I escaped the paralysis that came from life's unexpected outcomes. As I write this book, I am living through yet another unexpected outcome—an unexpected outcome of strong betrayal and misrepresentation. A disruptor of life. I am certainly not immune to the polarizing effects of life's traumas. But, I do not get stuck for any length of time. Trauma is the great educator. It's an education we don't sign up for but one that propels us to greater heights, becoming people of greater depth. I am currently maneuvering through this disruptor with surprising strength, clarity, trust, and bounce-back ability. If not for wisdom gained! Proverbs 1:7 (NIV) says, "The fear of the Lord is the beginning of knowledge, but fools despise wisdom and instruction." The fool learns nothing from experience.

The journey out of paralysis is not for the faint of heart. You will have to depend on the power of a God bigger than you for tenacity, bounce-back ability, and perseverance. There is work to be done. But, within the work a faith journey will ensue. That faith journey promises that God is on the scene before we ever even experience the unexpected happening. Existing within this space of faith will allow you to receive from an innate force, there to shore you up for the work ahead.

The minute the surgeon walked out of the room, I called my husband and said, "Get to the hospital now. They are talking about my chances of ever walking again and about transporting me to Health South Hospital for God knows how long. What is happening? What happened? Could it be malignant? Why hasn't anyone told me that there is a problem? What happened to the two- or three-hour surgery and three days in the hospital?"

I remember truly starting to come unraveled. Those first twenty-four hours were a nightmare. They had me heavily sedated, but I remember touching my torso and feeling like I had been cut off from my breast down. It was terrifying, and if not for the sedation of the drugs I would have been in a full-blown panic attack.

Later that morning, two super kind OR staff members stopped by. They said, "We just wanted to pop in and see how you were doing. Our shift ended in the middle of your surgery due to the unexpected extended time in the OR, and we were anxious for an update." As my foggy brain was trying to process, I was thinking, "Oh my gosh there was a shift change before my surgery ended?"

A male nurse came in with the assignment of getting me up on the portable toilet. Fear must have been radiating off of me. I couldn't feel anything and was trying to make sense of the terror of sitting up while not feeling three quarters of my body. Attempting to use the toilet while that portion of my body felt nonexistent dumbfounded me. The sheer helplessness I felt was overwhelming. Where was the body that had performed at such a high level for forty years? I cried from terror and the lack of physicality. The nurse's next response sent my brain into a dismal state of despair. "Don't worry, my wife is quadriplegic, and we have been married for many years. I know just how to work with you." Oh my God in heaven. Why was he referring to me and quadriplegia in the same sentence? My brain was scrambled. And, as if God knew the very minute I would hit a dismal wall of despair, a female nurse entered the room.

She stood by my bedside, and as we looked at each other, we realized we knew each other from a church Greg and I were visiting and had attended only a handful of times. She held my hand as I began to vent to her. My recollection of the conversation is not completely clear, but her countenance told me that she could see the fear and confusion I was feeling. I began to tell her all that had transpired and how the plan did not turn out as expected. All the questions and concerns began to pour out as she held my hand. She said, "Let's pray together." That woman entered as a messenger from my Father, and peace entered the room through her prayer. It was so clear that her timing was not coincidence. I wish I could remember her name from Austin Stone Church, working in the Seton ICU in November of 2007. I wish she knew how God used her in such perfect timing. We prayed. I cried. She comforted me.

My precious friends showed up that afternoon to visit me in the ICU. These were my cheerleaders. The ones praying, loving, and secretly collecting. They were collecting money for Greg and me. Going into surgery, I knew Greg was a train wreck about money, as our deductible was incredibly high. The night prior, as they stood by my bedside, I mentioned—in my morphine stupor—how bad I felt about the responsibility he was carrying. The financial and construction markets were crashing, and now we would owe $10,000 for my surgery. For months, he had been caring for Lauren and me and certainly there was more of that coming.

These friends standing bedside in the ICU were the same friends who were in the room when the surgeon came out to brief everyone on the unexpected outcome that had transpired on the surgical table. After seeing me in the ICU, they left the hospital to have dinner and make a plan. The next afternoon, they appeared with huge smiles and at least five boxes, attached together, from smallest to largest, to form a tower. In one box was pajamas, in another were magazines, in another were body products and a hair and nail makeover for when I got home, in the last smallest box was the money for the deductible! Literally, within twenty-four hours these girls showed up with the deductible in full. It was literally a miracle. The hands and feet of Jesus.

Greg had arrived and was standing off to the corner of the room. As soon as I realized what they had done, I turned to him and tried to express how grateful I was for all that he had done to serve me that year. Two tons of weight must have washed off of him as I was able to hand the envelope to him and say, "Maybe this will help the financial burden. It's the least that I (we) could do."

There was one other gift, and as I opened the box, my girlfriends shrieked, "These are your goal! You have to get back into your heels! Sit them right here in the window and look at them every day. You are going to get back into your heels, Amy!" The box held red patent-leather high-heeled shoes. They knew me. They knew I was a high-heeled shoe girl. Up until surgery I wore heels, platforms, pumps, you name it. I even often walked properties with my builder husband in a pair of super cute burlap platforms! The fact that I'd packed away forty-plus pairs of high-heeled shoes was very upsetting. Once a shoe girl, always a shoe girl. I did not own one pair of flats until earlier in the year when the pain set in. I reluctantly bought them because they were all I could wear.

After everyone left, my husband and I had a really tough conversation about the condition I was in. He said the surgeon was quite sure the tumor was benign; it had been growing for so long that it would have killed me already had it been malignant. Still under the influence of a heavy dose of morphine, I had a short period of time to process all that Greg was saying. During this brief window, something happened that changed the entire trajectory of my outcome. I began to resolutely profess, "I am a runner! I do not want to just walk; I want to run. *I am a runner!*"

The red shoes from my girlfriends quickly became famous. They graced the windowsill of each room I moved to over the next few months, and each new nurse would say, "Wow nice shoes" or "What's up with those shoes?" or "Love those red shoes" or "I'm going to take those red shoes girl!" I obviously had to tell each new set of nurses the story behind them, and I would repeat each time, "That's a goal, that's a goal, that's a goal." Cheerleaders—you cannot do life without them.

SOULED OUT

The first time in my life when I souled out, I was in my neighborhood, standing in the middle of the street, on the morning of my thirtieth birthday. I can still feel the Austin, Texas humidity on that hot August morning. I had hit my internal rock bottom, landing myself in the ER—not once but twice—with alcohol poisoning. The humiliation and degradation of those incidents jolted me toward a radical repentance, and a decision I made that morning in the middle of the street turned the tide of my life. The running joke had always been that I chose drugs over alcohol more often than not because I was way better at using drugs that drinking.

My life, on the outside at least, looked like a raving success. I was making six figures in my twenties as a sales executive, driving a fancy sports car, and eating great sushi with regularity. But the internal turmoil of the previous twenty years of self-compromise, shallow living and an aching soul that resulted from extremely sad experiences were closing in on me. The need to set a new standard for my life had been brewing, and these ER incidents proved without a shadow of a doubt it was time to raise the bar for my life and my future. Repentance turns the tide. I was done with the way it had been. I needed and desired total freedom—the kind that brings healing to the soul! Heading down the street for my morning run, I began a conversation with God that was long overdue.

"God, I've made a mess of my life. My twenties have been internal torture. I'm aching inside from all that has happened to me and I cannot get my life right. God, I've done it all my way and it is not working. I give all of me over to all of you. You get the next ten years of my life. Do it your way. Whoever does the better job with their decade gets the rest of my life!" (You know God was loving this deal!) I souled out! My mind, my will, and my emotions were surrendered to a life of faith with Christ as the core. The decision that morning, the professing from my mouth and the dedication that followed, changed the fiber of my existence.

God won about two years into our "deal." Pressing into that new standard meant immersing myself in habits that would recalibrate my standard of living. Those habits included habitual prayer, association with a new friend group, deep study of The Word, and pouring out in worship. I have come to coin that as a winning formula: W^2P^2 (Word, worship, prayer, people). The processes of surrender, forgiveness, and inner healing also took place in order for lasting change to occur. And, truth be told, a supernatural level of grace that only God can extend rocked me to my core. I learned that true Christianity is about freedom, not rules and regulations but grace, acceptance, and love. And, lucky for me, third, fourth, and even fifth chances to get things right. My next-level life arrived in the form of soul freedom.

The second time I souled out was in the ICU at the age of forty-one. I souled out to running, not just walking. If there were anything I knew that I knew, it was that I was made to move. I was that ever-moving child, the cheerleader, the drill team member, the runner, and the basketball player. The day I delivered my baby girl through emergency C section I was scheduled to teach an aerobics class. That day in the ICU, I made the DECI-

SION that *I was made to move.* I began to DECLARE it to all those surrounding me *who were committed to the success of my journey.* I DEDICATED *myself, no matter the cost and without knowing the future.* You are about to learn how to radically change the outcome of your own paralysis through the power of decision, declaration, and dedication! It is not as much about effort as it is about epiphany and mindset.

There were other times in my life when this approach delivered me from paralysis—the paralysis and roadblocks that alcohol, drugs, promiscuity, fear of man, guilt, shame, anxiety, and depression all establish in one's life, in *my* life. Many years prior, each of these demons had attempted to derail me in reaching my destiny. All of these tormenters attacked my true self, my free self, my joy-filled, love-filled self. This approach worked to help me conquer all the debilitating thoughts of *Am I Enough? Can I really do this? Will they take me seriously? Will I live through this? Am I smart enough to move up? Will I ever really belong? Will I ever be loved?*

Through all of those experiences I had to **make a decision** about who and what I was going to be and the direction I was going. Had I not taken each of those steps, I would not be standing here (literally) today. I had to **declare it** to those dedicated to the success of my journey, which enabled my mental and spoken story to change. Finally, I resolved to **dedicate myself** no matter the cost and without knowing the future, which is where the concept of putting in the work came into play.

Becoming Souled Out requires a decision-declaration-dedication approach from the deepest part of ourselves. It is an act of will to purpose our mind, will, and emotions to be laser focused on living the life we were born to live and laser-focused on the giver of life. Laser-focused on all that He is and all that He makes available to us in that moment of becoming souled out. *Selling out* is the cheap counterfeit of becoming *souled out.* In becoming souled out, there is substance and passion, whereas in selling out, there is lack and compromise. There is a denial of your truth. Your core knows the difference, and the instant you sell out, your mind, will, and emotions begin suffering through a battle that cannot be won. When we sell out to the demands and dictation of this world, we suffer both internally and externally. Our heart, soul, spirit, and physical body ooze sickness and suffer paralysis. I think that, many times, the definition of chronic stress can simply be stated as "I have sold out." When you have *souled* out, however, to the resonance of your core, it reflects an "adding unto" from which point momentum and roots begin to take hold. Positive energy begins traveling to an ordained destiny, not a cheap and shallow alternative.

When I formed Souled Out Ministries (a 501c3) in 2009, it was founded on this exact shift in the way one can live life—"sell out" versus "souled out." The concept was the original brainchild for both the ministry and the path to spiritual freedom.

Your soul. Your deepest most inner self. You cannot see it, but you can feel it, you can sense it. It is innately inside of you. It has been knocked around, shot down, and turned upside down. It has been lied to, it has been deceived, it has been detoured. But it doesn't go down without a fight. For many, it has also been nurtured and encouraged. It rumbles every now and then in an attempt to remind you of the good, of who you were before life placed you in a vice grip. To remind you of what it was like before loss and hurt seized your heart and mind. Unexpected outcomes can choke out the soul or raise it to new heights. The health of it is of utmost importance in freely reaching the next-level life you desire.

After my physical paralysis, I quickly realized that the processes I applied were exactly the way to gain massive success in both life and business. Through applying the "souled out" principles, I was able to achieve top earning salesperson status within months of coming on board a new sales team. And this was *after* having been out of the workforce for many years and after having gone through physical paralysis.

I formed Souled Out Ministries as an outreach ministry to help women break the chains that bind their abilities and beliefs. It launched as a faith-based, prime-time morning radio show that I hosted, Monday through Friday, and as an organization that hosted inner healing events. Our team hosted weekend events that walked women out of oppression of any kind and into freedom so that they could get on with their next-level life both personally and professionally. Just before the nonprofit's launch, I went away to a friend's cabin where I could think and listen. One of the questions I posed to myself and to God was, "What does 'souled out' really mean?" There in that cabin I waited for wisdom to speak, and when returning home from that weekend, I had in my possession thirty-one statements that defined what it means to become souled out.

They are truths to stand on and live by attached to faith. The statements start and end with the same declaration, which is "Becoming souled out means being human but staying the course." This statement means simply that even though we exist in a fallible human state, we stay the course. Staying the course implies that we are always doing the work that leads us to a life that is souled out and free. It means that even though we exist as fallible in our human condition with all our trips, slips, and falls, we can still be seeking a next-level life within which we will be experiencing massive success. *It is living life on purpose*! Yes, we can live both souled out and free. We can be free and not fractured.

And so it was, in the ICU, that I became souled out and something radically important resonated deep within my core. I souled out to the decision established long before that day in the hospital that I was made to move. *In that moment in the ICU, something powerful happened: My directives were set for mobility.*

Let's take a deep dive into the significance of establishing **decision, declaration, and dedication** in all different attempts to walk out of the wheelchair life has placed you in. The next few chapters will launch you towards your next-level life. Once the foundation is laid for getting unstuck and attaining new levels of success, we will jump back into the details of my miraculous story.

DECISION

t was the first day out of the ICU and inside the rehab hospital. The nurses entered and began following doctor's orders, organizing my room. The first thing out of my mouth was, "Where are the therapists? We need to get going! My goal is to run the Turkey Trot 5K next year." This annual race had just happened in downtown Austin and I professed, "I want to run that race this time next year!"

One of the nurses, who didn't seem like she was a runner at all, said, "Okay, honey, that's a good goal to have! I'll run that Turkey Trot with you." There I was, a paraplegic who had been in the rehab hospital for less than twelve hours, and I was proclaiming a decision that my main goal was to run within twelve months. I think the nurse probably felt safe in not having to fulfill her promise, but she was trying to be kind and encouraging, nonetheless. The other nurse moved towards the window and pulled back the curtains to let in the morning light. There they were—my red high-heeled shoes. "What are these?" she asked.

Let's start talking about decision by clarifying the type of decision that I am alluding to when I reference it throughout this book. We make dozens upon dozens of decisions every day. In fact, it is estimated that we make more than 30,000 decisions every single day. Why is it important to live a healthy lifestyle that is souled out to the things truest to our core? Because the conditions under which we make those 30,000 decisions can railroad our lives to the point where we end up living in endless chaos. The one decision I am referring to is the rare decision we make that involves resolve and creates the course for the other 29,999 decisions!

Can you absorb the fact that we make that many decisions, often with a poor state of mind, twenty-four hours a day, seven days a week? I created a word that clearly defines this type of decision: resolvolution. A resolvolution of the heart, soul, and spirit is a state of determination where resolve and revolution collide. Now that is a real decision!

The definition of resolve is "to decide firmly on a course of action. Settle or find a solution to (a problem, dispute, or contentious matter). Sort out, solve, work out." I love all of these appropriate synonyms. The decision I was making was to settle a contentious matter or fix and workout the truth that I was made to move. I was certainly made to walk, and I was claiming one rung higher, which was to someday run.

The second part of the word, revolution, is defined as "a forcible overthrow of a government or social order, in favor of a new system." I like the part about a forcible overthrow *in favor of a new system*. This can literally happen in your brain, and I can show you how. Synonyms for revolution are rebellion, uprising, and mutiny. When I experience a resolvolution of the heart, as with the decision I made in the ICU, it definitely has the power of an uprising or mutiny against the possibility that I was permanently wheelchair-bound.

Your life ebbs and flows with decisions of varying importance and depth. But, when there comes a time in our lives when we feel paralyzed, we must make a resolvolution of the heart—a decision that we refuse the lack, bondage, handcuffs, and barricades that have been set before us and within us. A decision that says, "This is the way I am going, and nothing but nothing will stop me from attaining my freedom, discovering what lies within the trauma, and the way out." In this decision phase, binary thinking must get rooted and grounded. (Yes, I do appreciate the times we should reflect, weigh our options, and consider them, but right now we are talking about walking out of a wheelchair).

Out-of-paralysis decisions either do or do not contribute to my here and now story. Not the story of the past and not the story of the future but the story of the present. Living in the past or the future when you are IN the present is paralyzing!

Powerful resolve is the key to loosening the grip of paralysis. Within the scope of this type of decision, you have to passionately care about the end results. It begins with first a simple thought, then a stirring of the heart. The mind and heart, once aligned, are ready for the positive emotion that propels action, which leads to success. It is a process. Trust the process.

If Biblical examples help, Daniel and his mighty men were one with their no-compromise standards. Esther, who even until death, made a decision to save her people. Her resolve: my people are not going to die! Paul, without wavering, made the decision to serve in the face of great adversity. His resolve: I will follow Christ regardless!

Next you must ignore the odds against you and prepare for adversity. Hang on to Proverbs 24:16: "For though the righteous fall seven times, they rise again, but the wicked stumble when calamity strikes." I once read an article that asked, "How many times should you get up after being knocked down? Once, twice, three times? How about until you're dead." And that, my friends, is a mic drop moment. Not once, not twice, but until you are dead. A decision made with resolvolution is a decision of epic proportions, and these sorts of decisions do not show up in life too terribly often. The resolvolution creates a culture that fuels stamina—the necessary process of action, adjust, action, adjust, and so on.

Resolvolution is accomplished when maturity takes over and you determine you will not live the wrong life any longer. Not roadblocked, not stuck, not locked down. If one strategy doesn't work, wrack your brain to find another. And another. And another. That is exactly what I have done for the past twelve years as I purposed to fulfill a decision made long ago. The processing of finding another strategy and then another is what I call "resourcing yourself." We will cover the concept in detail in the chapter about how to show up.

There were only one or two times when I deviated from this decision. It was absolutely the times when my mind veered and misaligned with my will that negative emotions were created. When left unattended, left to ruminate, the ship starts to stray. Resolve is the fuel that drives the engine of accomplishment. And, make no mistake, resolve does not mean "want to." Resolve involves massive action, where as "want to" does not. There are other elements to this method of success, but there is an order to the elements, and they must begin with resolve. I watched people in the hospital make the mistake of allowing their resolve to fade when they failed to accomplish their recovery goal *in a particular timeframe. But, people who succeed often do so because they continue on past the point where they expected to already have succeeded.*

I saw the phenomenon at play both in my own life and in the lives of others. I was told by the surgeon that at the five-year mark, we would know the extent of what would be left with regard to disrupted mobility and pain. As that year approached, the plan was to assess where we were so far and accept that as my fate. At year five, I was *so far* from where I wanted to be that I let that year come and go without giving it much thought. I refused to allow my mind to agree with expectations well below the standard I had set for mobility. My mind was focused on results regardless of what year had come and gone. As I write this book in year twelve, I remain committed to my initial decision.

I heard from the nurses time and time again, "People just quit, Amy." False expectations are set, and when they are not met, we quit. That happens a lot, even if only subconsciously. Especially when unexpected outcomes enter onto the scene. We get deflated, lose focus, and our decision begins to waiver. We engage with a self-limiting belief that says, "I should have already...it should have happened by now...I should have accomplished it by now...Now that this has happened, nothing will work" This all stems from a mind unattended. So, what is the cure for this? Unravel the self- limiting belief, unravel the meaning you attached to it, change your story, apply a simple brain technique, and you are on your way to a radical new way of life.

Within the subject of the decision that becomes a resolvolution of the heart, we must rope in the ideas of focus and clarity. It seems obvious, but we have all been sabotaged by a lack of one or both at one time or another. It could very well be the reason you cannot currently move yourself towards your goals. Become a master of focus. This is where clarity comes and perspective is adjusted. Within my online course, I guide you through exercises that set your focus on fire. Focus is a habit, and within that habit, clarity abounds. Perspective then gets a reality check and you are on your way out of lockdown.

Over the last twelve years, as it pertains to regaining my physical mobility, I can think of only a very small percentage of time when I focused on what I *did not* want. What I mean is, my mind, will, and emotions in the ICU got attached to and laser-focused on walking and running. I never headed to therapy thinking about what I did *not* want. I wanted to lift my right leg. The focus was not on the fact that I rarely could (which could honestly become maddening.) I focused on conquering the squat, not on the fact that I had to do it with balance poles (which could really hack me off.)

Unfortunately, there were times when I looked at what I vehemently did not want. Over the years, it's occurred when the pain got unmanageable and it infuriated me. Other times, I fixated on not being able to roller blade or wakeboard. I felt so cheated. Or, I got focused on my right-side abs that I lost most control of. The nerves made my stomach feel as if it was bigger, tighter, and more protruded than it was. It burned like crazy and measured two sizes bigger in clothes than the rest of my body. I love fashion, and it was a nightmare finding clothes that looked appropriate (and that I felt comfortable in). Then there was the day when I was congratulated and asked in the Barnes and Noble checkout line when I was due. For the record, I just ran with it saying. "Yeah, thanks, we are really excited! About five months," quickly assessing that my stomach resembled about a four-month-along bump!

Every time, the heaviness of that negative focus zapped my energy for the things I *could* do. I became aware that I was focusing on the "not," and it was becoming debilitating, both mentally and emotionally. When I was in that place, I was so low and so down on myself. So, I began letting the pain cues remind me of what I *did* want. For my abdominal issue, when I felt the negative trigger, I would automatically draw my abs in and re-member the end goal. To this day, I am still not great at that one, but my awareness keeps me in check.

We get focused on what we do *not* want out of life, that is exactly what we get. There is a great story of how a whitewater rafting guide was able to guarantee his patrons that they would not have an accident when the waters were high from rains that sent the rapids roaring. He said, "Here is what I tell my custom-ers. Watch my hand, and wherever you see it pointing towards, focus all your energy in that direction and paddle your faces off." He learned that if he told his patrons, "Don't hit the tree!" or "Don't go towards that giant boulder!" that is exactly where they would go. They went where they were focusing.

Many years ago, my husband (at the time) and I owned a boat and loved wakeboarding on Lake Austin. We were super into it, so we signed ourselves up for lessons so we could get even better. My turn came and the instructor said, "Get out there and wakeboard, and I will see why you are crashing so often." When I got back in the boat, he said, "You've got just one problem. Your form is great, but every time you look down at the water—the place you do not want to end up—that is ex-actly where you go. Keep your eyes on top of the water. Get your eyes off the place you *don't* want to go and you will stop crashing so often!" Best wakeboarding money ever spent.

You get more from what you look at, so you'd better be dead certain of what you want. Train your brain to find what is working, and then look at it harder and deeper.

As Dr. Leaf, author of *Who Switched Off My Brain,* explains (and I'm paraphrasing), you are what you think and will become what you think. The more you think about something, the more it controls you. Why? Because as you think, you are building memory and reinforcing existing memory and linking networks in your mind. You are literally growing new branches on what are called memory trees, and your brain has an unlimited capacity for growing these connections.

When addressing the subject of decision this thoroughly, we have to take a quick look at *indecision*. I recently discovered from my own experience that indecision is a habit. Indecision is allowing your brain to take an indefinite lunch break. Let's look at the indecisive habit of staring into space or at the wall. There are obviously other reasons for staring while in a numb brain state beyond indecision, including dehydration and food allergies. But let's talk about it from a habit and neuroscience standpoint.

This habit attached itself to my life on again and off again for many years. It began, understandably, through multiple traumatic unexpected outcomes that seemingly kept on coming. We have a built-in meter that protects us when a chronic state of pain, loss, or fear sets in. It's a sign that our brain is overwhelmed. The stress of those situations creates a numb brain state—or, at very least, mild to severe brain fog. This state makes clear decisions difficult to make. The key in my life was that it was happening *after* the traumatic situations had been somewhat remedied or after I'd moved past them. In other words, I wasn't deep in the fire at the moment, but the switch that had flipped my brain off during the crisis didn't switch back on. I started to recognize and acknowledge that the effects of indecision were numbing, polarizing, *and* habitual. And, I had allowed it to continue, assuming I had little control over it, which wasn't true.

Do you find yourself often staring at the wall in a state of numb indecision? If you typically allow your brain to sit numb when it is decision time, you can change that. You either need to address the stress surrounding decision time or the habit to go numb that has been formed over time. Perhaps you are engaged in a situation that gives rise to negative or unaligned belief systems you put in place long ago. When those stored memories are triggered, by related or unrelated information, your brain fires those responses back as if the previous trauma were happening all over again. Maybe yours is "What if I make a wrong decision?" or maybe you are faced with two optional paths and your brain goes in to panic mode, thinking, "I don't know which way to go!" We dial this scenario back in The Freedom Success Method™. There are simple solutions for replacing and redeciding some of the stored thoughts that are causing a numb brain state.

Procrastination is a long word for indecision, and it's a form of keeping your brain numb. Maturity identifies procrastination in our lives as a symptom of a greater problem: fear. The only way to kill fear is to take action. That *is* the antidote. And, it is a solution to the above-mentioned "numb brain" habit or condition. We never move forward chained to anything, and we cannot stay planted in place hoping for something better. Release must occur.

Take some time to sit with this. Ask yourself what fear is keeping you in indecision, and write down the answer you hear or sense. You might ask what old belief system is getting triggered that is shutting down your decision-making ability and write that down. Now, do that same thing five more times, asking from the new answer you get each time. Go five levels deep, and you will find the *real* reason. Release it, and let it go, fully into space, fully into the hands of God. Replace it with a truth that resonates with your current life plan. Whether you believe that what you discover owes you little or owes you everything, it owes you nothing. When we release a debt or comfortable-yet-debilitating belief system, we are truly free. You cannot stay stuck. You will begin coming out of paralysis.

Many times, indecision comes when the risk appears to be too high to make a decision. The problem is that there are risks in making decisions, and there are risks in *not* making decisions. Life is a risk! Walking out of paralysis comes with trial and error full of risk. Not making a decision to pursue mobility causes you to run the risk of never truly living in that area of your life.

In my own life, I have battled with another form of indecision. This habit, which can become a syndrome, is that of perfectionism. Perfectionism is paralyzing. I have done the work, and I am walking out of this "wheelchair!" But, perfectionism keeps you waiting for eternity to make a decision because of the land of "not." Perfection keeps decisions dead. It is fear-based and has no place in the life of a mobility master, which is what you and I both want to become. I'm learning that it is not about being perfect; it is about getting the job done with measurable results. Your behavior should look like this: take action, test results, adjust, go again. Repeat, repeat, repeat. Growth from action brings exhilaration to our lives.

We want the next-level life where we are closer to our God designed destiny, and unhindered by roadblocks. I had to get to the place in my life where I was sick and tired of this debilitating habit of perfectionism. Honestly, I had come to hate it, but I did not know the way out.

There were two ways I finally did get out. First, I hired an accountability coach to check me on it every week. It was some of the best money I've ever spent. Hiring a coach *solves the problem* of paralysis in a multitude of circumstances. A stuck project, a stuck mind, a stuck relationship, the need for momentum, the need for clarity, the need to continue in excellence. Second, I came to the truth that *progress would be my perfection*. Taking steps forward, as imperfect as I might label them, would be my "perfect." Once I grasped that, I wrote a book, further developed a radio program, and built my dream company—all within a year.

Perfectionism is like an addiction. You loathe the aftermath but just can't quit. Look, I love excellence. I have always strived for excellence in everything I do. It has paid off for me, and it is a way of life I am proud of and choose. *But*, there is a fine line between excellence and perfectionism. In excellence, we thrive and succeed. In perfectionism, we live in the land of indecision, in the spin cycle, if you will. There is no more time for a "spin cycle life" in Jesus's name, child!

DECLARATION

One of the fastest girls in junior high, I must have put a million miles on my bicycle. Long brown hair flowing behind my back as the wind danced through it, banana seat, hot pink straws covering the spokes, fringe dancing from the handlebars. I ran track, played basketball, and adored my cheerleading team. I was considered one of the better athletes as a young person.

My summer and fall job during high school was at the local recreation department as a coach for youth T-ball, basketball, and girls softball. I'm not entirely sure exactly when I started running for sport, but I must have been young enough that I can't remember the age I was. Track meets were an integral part of my life growing up, and drill team was added in high school to my athletic enthusiasm. I was awarded often for my zeal, enthusiasm, and smile.

God was there. He was everywhere. My mother made sure of it. Little did I know I would still be running the streets of whatever neighborhood I lived in some twenty-five years later. I think I gravitated to running because it was the thing that allowed me to expend the most energy. All of that energy! What a saint my mom was to manage my energy, coupled with the spirit of adventure I was born with. Mother always honored the passion I had for running and the therapeutic purpose it served in my life. For years, a staple of my Christmas wish list was new running shoes. Up until she passed, mother expected that after coffee and an early morning visit at the kitchen table, I would be heading out the door for my run.

And then, there I was, lying in the ICU with my declaration that I was a runner. It would have been counterintuitive to my soul to believe for anything less. It would have been thoroughly out of alignment to profess anything less. My declaration overrode the implication that merely walking was the goal.

In a matter of hours *all those committed to the success of my healing journey* knew the bar had been set. The standard was actually set even before I went under the knife. This declaration was as much for me and my brain "set point" as it was for everyone else. It was "go" time! The decision had taken root and the proclamation was emphatic. I was made to move, and I wanted to run, not just walk! I did not rush to Google to research statistics on how rare this condition was and how few people who have it ever walk again. I did not mix in with my decision and declaration the what ifs. We were talking about paralysis, and I wanted out.

For many of you, paralysis includes roadblocks that have stolen away and limited you for decades. Maybe you are a high achieving individual who has had success but who has also become a master at masking points of paralysis. Perhaps the mask is there because you have no idea how to get yourself free. Nevertheless, you know there is a next-level life just outside your front door.

Walking again is serious business! Take pause here and reflect on the fact that our declarations, our new stories intended to align with where we are headed, aren't for everyone. Notice, I declared my intentions to *all those committed to the success of my journey*. Sometimes it behooves us to keep our mouths shut.

Honestly. Stop trying to beg people to buy into your new story. There are people who are not going to be committed to the success of your journey. There are people who will scoff at your new story because it challenges their old story. There are people who will not be able to get behind your declaration simply because they are stuck in a response mode of negative overdrive – and they don't even know it. Forgive them. Don't allow that to become yet another sticking point you have to get past. Many times, their resistance towards you *is* the sticking point. *Because* of the chain others have tethered us to, we haven't been able to accomplish the kind of movement that leads to success. There are many examples, but one I cope with is a person in my life who is all in with me when I am in crisis, but when I start to soar and succeed or excel to new places, they turn bitter, biting, and downright resentful. In order to utilize your declaration to the fullest, detach your emotions from and temper your reactions to those not buying into your new story. This process of walking out of the wheelchair life has placed you in must include disregarding people's adverse comments and unexpected reactions to your new story, your new declaration.

I am still not immune to people I care about having adverse opinions on how I decide and declare to get myself out from behind roadblocks. My more than fair share of past mistakes and bends in the road have jaded their instinctive responses. I get it. But this is my life, my destiny. I either free myself and live the next-level life I feel stirring in my bones, or I cower to people's comments and false beliefs about who I am or who I should be.

The percentage of people I have helped who were stuck because other people cast their own self-limiting beliefs upon them is far too high! People's opinions are polarizing. Remember, their opinions are coming from the eyes of their experiences (or lack thereof). And, honestly, the people's opinions that hurt me the most came out of their own brokenness and judgement. Moral of the story: The act of getting mobile again is going to take soul alignment. That alignment allows for zero percent of your energy to go to anything counter to your declaration.

One of the most paralyzing elements in our lives is aligning early on with a story that is not our birthright. What story are you declaring that misaligned your mind, will, and emotions (soul) and brought paralysis. These stories live in our subconscious mind and are constantly dictating direction—or lack thereof. The Freedom Success Method™ is about observing where the story went wrong. The discovery process identifies when the story became counterintuitive to who you are in your truest form. Was it an imposed belief system? Was there a proclamation made about you or over you that your mind recorded? When you adopt any of these (which we all tend to do unknowingly, unless it is a determination or vow we make), your emotions followed, and you went into fight-or-flight mode and got stuck there. The belief or behavior you adopted is often not what you would expect, and this discovery is a game changer.

Several levels deep, almost everyone is blocked at one time or another (or always) by "I am not enough" or "What I want in life I cannot have" or "I am on the outside looking in." The Freedom Success Method™ addresses those sticking points and the reasons you are fighting yourself or those around you. It also uncovers why you ran and hid and lost your voice. There is an innate alignment that sets you free to excel. It explains your fear and moves you to a state of fear-less-ness! In case you are unaware, God made a point to say, "Fear not!" 365 times in the Bible! A reminder every single day. If you are disillusioned about the fact that your life should add up to more than it currently does, allow me to help you find your new story.

We have to create a new story. Wherever you are today, you likely need a new story to get you where you want to be. Are you stuck on a story? The story that got you out of Egypt is not the story that will get you to the promised land! But, because, can't, didn't, they are not, I am not, he did, she didn't, I did, I didn't... Those stories come from other failures or false belief systems.

In creating a new story, you are dismantling barriers. Stay away from things that create a story as to why you cannot come out of lockdown. Run from anything that aligns with your limiting belief story. Everyone has one! Why are you listening to other paralyzed people? Why are you happy-houring with people who are in lockdown, paralyzed, stifled? (I'm not referring to those in need of your love and help. I'm referring to your inner circle and those who influence you.) *Change your story, change your life.*

The enemy of your soul gathers up knowledge of bad experiences and influences you with it to the degree that you make a vow or determination or lie and play it over and over deep within your mind. And, if you give it thought long enough, it affects genetic expression. Yes, your DNA expression can be altered. It keeps you stalled out, stuck, and paralyzed WITHIN THAT STORY instead of allowing you to learn from it as an observer and then moving forward. In my online course, I teach you how to identify when that story took root, bust it up, and get the new story to stick and stay. There is meaning attached to every story.

The depth of the meaning you attached to the story that was carried forward dictates the amount of work that needs to be done to get mobile and headed in the right direction. In your brain, these memories look like trees with lots of branches. The thoughts you have ruminated over look like full, bushy tree branches, and they are cross-communicating with other knowledge and memories. This network has to be rewired. In other words, some of those trees need serious pruning in order to minimize the power they have in your life. This relatively new neuroscience proving neuroplasticity of our brain is fantastic news for you and me. Scientists can now observe the actual pruning of thought trees as it takes place! We can undo the negative effects and build upon the good.

So, how do we flip the script? First and foremost, we have got to know what the Bible says about our story. Jeremiah 29:11 tells you about your story. It involves hope and future, plans of prosperity, and neither fear nor harm. The word tells us who we are to be in Christ, which translates into who we are in our truest form, I talk to people a lot about hearing the voice of God because of my own experience with it.

The first thing I teach is this: How can you determine the voice of God in your life if you do not know God? You may know "of" God, but to truly know Him, we have to know His word, right? If I haven't gotten to know you, how do I, one, know your voice and, two, know if what I hear about you lines up with your character? Same concept comes into play when knowing what is true and in alignment as you begin to declare a new, more accurate story about who you are (your truest form) and what your destiny story is.

Next, we must adopt transformational vocabulary because our brain believes what we tell it. Get words involved that can be your focus, and you will start to experience these words. Positive feelings will follow, and this is where massive action begins to occur because your soul is now invested. Tony Robbins, one of the greatest motivators and experts on human success, talks about the truth that emotion drives decision and action. He goes on to explain that it is not skill or intellect that drives decision but emotion—because it's about pleasure and pain and whether you're seeking or avoiding them. This falls in line with the concept of humans not implementing change until there is a lot of pain inflicted. It is not a best practice, but it is human nature.

With regard to transformational vocabulary, let's agree that we speak and declare words over our lives all day, every day. *If emotion is a driver of action and that emotion is birthed from words, we must become an observer of our word habits.* We all have habitual word habits. What words do you observe consistently coming out of your mouth that are reconfirming paralysis over and over in your brain? Common examples are "No one ever notices or hears me" and "I will never figure this all out."

Words attach meaning; meaning creates emotion; emotions drive actions that we may or may not desire. Please stop for just a minute and consider this process in your own life. Are the actions being developed within this process the actions you desire? Or is the process producing the same debilitating result over and over and over again? The conclusion is, we are in need of changing the meaning we have applied to certain situations. Declaring the Word of God over our lives is the exact example of this. Our words change, therefore our brain changes, and before we know it our life is full of the Holy Spirit and producing positive change. Words have to change before freedom comes onto the scene. You cannot speak death, downcast, or negative words and produce life. Doing so is like planting potatoes and expecting cilantro!

A constant word used is a constant state of experience. Our words actually become our experience, whether they are accurate or not. Why? Because our brain believes what we say. Are lightbulbs starting to come on for you? Can you see how language is so powerfully directional?

However you represent the world to yourself in words or metaphors determines your experience. What are the words now and in the past that are getting in your way and presenting a barrier? These barriers built by words have to be removed or minimized so you can get what you really want out of life. Tony Robbins also often talks about metaphors we adopt that shape our outcome. Flippant speech is not flippant. For example, "I'm dying over this," "I am so sick," "I'm at the end of my rope," and "I am never going to get there." In my twenties, because of the chaos of my life I caught myself saying things such as "I feel crazy" and "I am going crazy." I was agreeing over and over with the instability of my life. Those words were searing the belief deeper and deeper into my brain for future use and to serve as future triggers. We literally hypnotize ourselves with words. Consider the metaphors that come out of *your* mouth a lot. Hint: they are buried within your story. Pick one or two right now that need to get aligned. Otherwise, you are creating more of the same crippling behavior from these words and metaphors.

As we continue to move through this chapter, let it be "declared" that I am not suggesting you live in *la la land* and turn a blind eye to situations. Many of you reading this are in the dead center of a mind-blowing, unexpected outcome. As I told my friend who recently shared her husband's cancer diagnosis with me, "We cannot deny that you are about to head down a really rugged path. You can't go around; you have to go through, but you can align right now what you say and declare over the stifling news." Intentional word selection can make for a much more bearable road.

Declarations, transformational words, and the creation of a new story are all about retraining your brain and your nervous system. Dr Caroline Leaf, a neuroscientist and my brain hero, teaches on this very subject. Dr Leaf is a devout woman of faith, and she has made it her life's mission to transform what we know about brain science and the way it confirms that we are surely created by an all- knowing God. I quote her often and share her transforming research whenever possible.

Dr. Leaf teaches that the accurate model for implementing lasting story redirection is to first acknowledge the negative habit, situation, or old story. She then says that one must redirect to the new desired outcome. This would be what you are wanting your brain to know, believe, and recall. It is that process of pruning and rebuilding trees that produce far better fruit. Using the metaphor from my twenties, my example would be, "Yes, this situation is making me feel crazy, but I am choosing to foster stable thoughts. From this day forward, I am sane and capable" or "Yes, I feel stuck right now and if feels horrible, but I will find the answers I am looking for and reach all my goals—and then some!" This practice eventually creates the tipping point toward a new direction, creating memory that serves us well. You are now preparing your brain for action towards stability. The shape your brain is in when unexpected outcomes befall you is the shape it will be in as you get through the ordeal. You may not be able to dictate the outcome (leave that to God), but you *can* dictate how you get through it. This brain training is DIRECTLY RELATED to our ability or inability to be resilient. So do it now, before the next unexpected outcome befalls you.

Resilience is one of my superpowers. We all have one or two superpowers or powerful gifts. This ongoing advantage in my life of having bounce-back ability comes from having a strong mental disposition plus hope plus faith. Overcomer status was built through three decades of maneuvering through unexpected outcomes. I learned of the desperate need to have a mind under control from a mind that was completely out of control. This is why soaking in the Word of God can produce such peace and direction. It is feeding your brain and soul non-stop truth, wise counsel, and inspiration. I keep doing the brain work and claiming my God-ordained destiny.

This superpower of resilience was honed during several trips to hell and back. I've endured hellish experiences that brought on roadblocks, lockdown, even physical paralysis. The journey from hell to home, however, is where the magic happened. The magic being the realization that much of my health on the other side of that particular experience came from realigning my thoughts through brain control. *Plus* renew, renew, renew, and be a seeker of truth. Romans 12:2 (NIV): "Do not conform to the pattern of this world but instead be transformed by the renewing of your mind. Then, you will be able to test and approve what God's will is—His good, pleasing, perfect will."

There are myriad destructive lies we have embedded in our minds, and as they surface, we can utilize this same process to acknowledge, replace, and build resilience for the future. That is brain science at work. *It is a kindergarten process with college level* discipline. The only thing standing between where you are and where you want to be is the story you tell yourself.

Start an awareness campaign. I did just that when my daughter was really young. One day, she told me straight up, "Mom, you complain a lot." That was a gut punch. It sickened me. I've prided myself on being positive (or so I thought.) She was right. All of that mouth junk was a mixture of excellence turned into "never enough." Perfectionism (which always stems from fear) began tipping the scale to judgement and other brain trash. Immediately, I set a new standard for my mouth and for my daughter! I did a pretty good job simply because of the awareness. I've always taught that *awareness is half the battle!*

We create an environment with our story that is cast upon, thrust upon, forced to marinate on our children. This word environment grows children who carry these self- limiting beliefs and negative mindsets before they even know what they are. I've seen with my own eyes this toxic word environment we create take root in a mom and daughter who are close to Lauren and me. The mom's ill alignment of her own soul brought out statements and judgements about Lauren and bathed her daughter's environment in it. Drip, drip, drip until a tipping point occurred and the daughter who literally adored Lauren now has a distasteful disposition toward her. I watched this happen over a number of years. The daughter isn't even really sure why she has disdain for Lauren; she just runs with it. To this day, I don't always get it right, but my awareness ensures that Lauren is in a healthy word environment.

Ten years later, God gently revealed the truth that I had created a toxic word environment for myself. The spirit of God took me through a journey of deep surgery to cut out yet another level of "not"—*It's not enough; it's not what I want; it's not, it's not, it's not.* I had reached a place in life of disillusionment and disappointment, some of it warranted, some of it not.

But either way, "not" was not the way out! God dove deep into my *awareness* and drove me to declarations to break the cycle.

For months, I would first catch the "not" thought, acknowledge its presence and how it was fueling negative emotions, and then apply a replacement thought. I came up with what I call "intervention words" and applied them until that is all I could hear, think, or say.

Many years before I learned anything about brain science and how God created all the systems attached, I was executing the concepts with success. It was during my spiritual revolution, just after I learned how the enemy had played me into his hand for a very long time. My sights were set on maximum freedom, and I launched an all-out assault on the enemy of my soul. It seemed that I would get diligent about a change in my life and then get distracted and re-ensnared. So, I got sticky notes, wrote on them the new behavior I had purposed, and placed them everywhere. It was in the day of day timers, so I had them in my day timer, on my bathroom mirror, on the refrigerator, and on the car dashboard. I deemed these my "sticky note campaigns" and they worked! Just about the time the new discipline would slip my mind, I would see a sticky note that would remind me and strengthen me. They were crazy successful, even though my husband thought I was nuts. But he liked the new me, so it all worked out.

A number of years ago, there was a movement within Christianity and particular ministries that got a really bad rap as a name-it-and-claim-it theology took over. Please hear the balance and Biblical truth I am about to share to prove that declaration out of our mouth or within our psyche is pivotal to huge success. Success that defies the odds. Isn't that what you are looking to do? Defy the odds before you?

Declarations help us call those things that are not as though they are. This is a God habit! *God, who gives life to the dead and calls those things which do not exist as though they did* (Romans 4;17). *God's method* of bringing life to dead places and paralyzed people is for someone to say it is alive when it still looks dead. What is faith anyway? To believe before we see, not to see in order to believe. Even non-believers do this, they just don't call it faith. When we declare things alive that look dead, we become like God in "calling those things that are not as though they are."

If I am paralyzed, locked down, or stuck, I am looking for life to come into that area of my life. Right? Life is in the power of the tongue. Proverbs 18:21 says that life and strength are accelerated through our declarations. Who out there needs an accelerated plan? Anybody? Am I the only one who wants every unfair advantage I can get to bring me some life up in this dead space? Words in agreement with God's Word will propel us into abundant life. A John 10:10 life. Abundance, mentally and emotionally. We will be able to enter the realm of our salvation as we make these declarations.

We believe what we say about ourselves more than anyone else does. Therefore, we should constantly hear ourselves saying words like blessed, healthy, strong, valuable, talented, and capable. The alternative is hearing ourselves saying things like "not enough," "not strong," "can't speak," "can't withstand," "shouldn't speak up"... Write down the words you hear yourself saying repeatedly—even if just in your mind (actually, *especially* if in your mind)—that you are getting hung up on the most. Do it right now. What are some adjectives you cannot believe about yourself? Ask why and listen for the answer. Ask where the word came from in the first place, and listen for the answer. Ask what it might take to change your mind. These questions start to bring up answers for your next-level life. Your awareness of them will begin a reset process. Stop trivializing the power of this process in your life.

There is a new realm within which to begin living if you want a next-level life. Now, what the heck does "realm" mean? The definition of realm, according to Webster-Merriam is "A royal jurisdiction or domain; a region that is under the dominion of a king; kingdom in particular with God's kingdom in the hearts and lives of believers." You cannot live within the realm of the earthly world and be expecting the freedom that comes from living within the realm of God. You reap the realm in which you sow!

You are on your way out of paralysis. Our declarations are instrumental for us to enter our promised land. In and of themselves, they are not the answer, but they must be in place to win. Why? Because your mouth is strategically agreeing with your mind, will, and emotions and your spirit is heading in the same direction as these guideposts you're putting in place. In the book of Judges, Joshua was instructed to implement nonstop speaking (declaring) of truth as he made final preparations to possess what God had already given through His promise: the promised land!

"This book of the law shall not depart from your mouth, but you shall meditate on it day and night that you may observe to do according to all that is written in it. For then you will make your way prosperous and then you will have good success" (Joshua 1:8) *The big takeaway here is that the use of declarations was not for God, it was for Joshua! To strengthen him and prepare him for a big win.*

Your mind believes whatever you tell it. Declarations are a way to overcome anxiety and become confident. "Anxiety in the heart of man causes depression, but a good word makes it glad" (Proverbs 12:25).

Joel Osteen, who leads Houston's Lakewood Church, which is now the largest congregation in the United States with over 40,000 members, often speaks and writes about the fact that what you speak out loud becomes cemented in your mind. He is sometimes accused of being the "positivity pastor," but with 40,000 plus members, it sounds to me like a lot of people need to hear a good "word" spoken over their lives. I thank God that he gave us a way to reverse established wrong alignment! Yes, it is way easier to avoid it in the first place than to have to reverse it, but at least adjustment and healing *can* be attained—if we do the work.

You have to send out words in the direction you want your life to go. You cannot talk about defeat and subsequently have victory. You cannot talk about lack and expect to have overflow. Where your focus goes (and grows), energy flows. Can you see the dis-ease within a person when their mind, will, and emotions are going in different directions? Then, add to that one's confused spiritual direction and health path, and you have a tangled polarized human being. Drained, frustrated, and confused. Helping individuals align all of these is the very passion of my heart!

My secret weapon to begin spiritual realignment: I am sharing with you a declaration that, for years, was taped to my bathroom mirror. It was repeated (out loud) hundreds of times within a two-year period. I got it from Shoreline Church when I was experiencing massive spiritual transformation. I have no idea who wrote it, but I adopted it as mine. It set my mind in a totally different direction from the realm I had been existing in (that I was stuck in!). This declaration played a transformative role in my becoming souled out. It was instrumental in turning my spiritual titanic around. You can build one for your business life, relational life, or spiritual life.

I AM
Who God Says I am,
A child of God
The righteousness of God,
Because I am born again.
I am sanctified and I'm full of the Holy Spirit,
Therefore,
I can do what God says I can do, and
I CAN DO
All things through Christ who strengthens me.
I will say what God says I can say,
Because His Word in my mouth produces FAITH
And greater is He that is in me,
Than he that is in this world.
So I now bind the devil and every demonic force
That has been dispatched against me, my family,
My pastors and their families.
IN JESUS' NAME I take my place,
I'm not just in the church—I am the CHURCH.
I now let loose the power of the Holy Spirit
To change my life, to change my heart
And to flow through me like never before.
COME HOLY SPIRIT
Interrupt the way I think,
Interrupt the way it has been.

I AM READY TO CHANGE
IN JESUS' NAME.

Don't use your words to remain snared in your current situation. Use your words to *change* your situation. Proverbs 6:2
says: "We are snared by the words of our mouth." The more we
talk about something, the more we draw it in. So, the transition
is, instead of talking about the problem, talk about the solution.

When my husband and I were wanting to get pregnant and
it was not happening, we began to profess, "Thank you for our
baby you have for us, thank you, thank you. We cannot wait for
this baby!" Day in and day out, we prayed this together out
loud. Not "Loooooorrrddd we want a baby. If it is your will let us
have a baby someday." Even after my miscarriage, which was so
painful, we continued to just declare and send energy into the
space into which we wanted life to come. (This does not mean,
by the way, that if you are not getting pregnant, your declaration is wrong. It is simply a great example of how we choose
declarations that are counter to what we are experiencing and
directed at what we want.)

Joel Osteen gives a declaration of "I know when one door
closes God will open another door. What was meant for my
harm God will use to my advantage. I'm not only coming out; I
will come out better off than I was before." You want freedom?
You've got to align your declaration with your mind, will, emotions, and spirit. If you can't pull this off, discovery has to occur,
and I can guide you through that process.

Come up with an "I declare" statement for yourself that
you can memorize and use as intervention (or turn into a sticky
note campaign). Then, visualize that statement over and over
until it becomes a belief. For years I used a portion of 2 Corin-

thians 10:5: "…I take captive every thought to make it obedient to Christ." It broke my brain from several toxic thought patterns that were thrusting me back into a depressive state. With interventions, before you know it, you'll have mobility in what was once a paralyzed space. Remember, He SPOKE the world into existence.

A ship gets turned around by a tiny rudder. Do you have a ship you need to turn around? Start with aligning words in the direction that the ship needs to be facing. Life is released by energy words, right words, words that line up and agree with God. You can start a revival of the heart with right words—an entire life can be turned around by the first-step implementation of right declarations. While it takes a minute to turn the titanic around, but it will turn. Be patient, and stay at the helm!

Do you want to be in this same place again next year…and then the next year…and then the next? I know you do not. Stand up, speak up, get your physiology behind it. Declaring is action, yet most people never get to that point.

We won't have something just by saying it, but saying something is necessary to having it. Build yourself up within the realm of the kingdom. Declaring is an action that will eventually move mountains.

Declaration does not produce a desired end result. It is the launch of the desired end result.

DEDICATION

The day after I arrived at the rehab hospital, I finally got a therapist to come to my room. As they sat me up on the side of the bed, my blood pressure crashed. I had developed orthostatic hypertension, a condition that causes your blood pressure to crash every time you rise due to being laid flat with inconsistent blood flow (due to lack of mobility). The "therapy" for this was to lay me on a tilt table and have the table raise at an incline until the blood pressure began to plummet, then level the table to flush and try again. This training continued until I was reconditioned to be able to tolerate a full upright position with regulated blood pressure. This was NOT the type of therapy I had in mind. My frustration level from losing precious time to get my body functioning again was enormous. I was ready to heal!

In one massive pivotal moment in the ICU, I *decided* that I was going to both walk *and* run. To accomplish this, *I would dedicate myself, no matter the cost and without knowing the future*. That dedication would prove to build an insatiable hunger in me that pressed through the all-consuming pain of walking out of paralysis.

What does that mean—to *dedicate yourself no matter the cost and without knowing the future*? It means that you do not have all the answers. It means you cannot see what lies ahead. It means that there may be high highs and low lows, but regardless, you are still ALL IN. It means that the *outcome is so crucial* that you are committing everything you have within you. The opposite path would have cost me everything. Have you thought about the cost of *not* dedicating yourself to getting out of the spin cycle?

Dedicate myself no matter the cost and without knowing the future means you and I are ready to shoulder the brunt of getting out of lockdown because the alternative is no longer an option. It also means that an exorbitant amount of faith and reliance on a higher power is ever-present. *No matter the cost and without knowing the future* means accepting that an omnipotent God must carry you when you cannot carry yourself.

Dedication that possesses a roaring hunger, which is needed when coming out of paralysis, is birthed from clarity. Clarity of where you are and where you are going. While clarity initially comes in the decision phase, the phase of dedication is where you begin to produce results. The results come out of the obsession for getting yourself to take action, adjust, take action, adjust in a new and unfamiliar space.

Do you find yourself in a predicament you have never been in before? I get it! I had never been paraplegic! Dedication no matter the cost and without knowing the future builds courage. It's putting yourself on the field and taking risk after risk after risk. Does that scare the heck out of you? If so, for a moment become an *observer* of your life, and it will become clear there are a multitude of activities you already engage in and give no thought to that are subject to risk. Life is one big risk. Your dedication can become louder than the voice of *what ifs* with clarity and positive emotion on board. What if I fail? What if it doesn't work? Risk. Risk. Faith. Faith. Faith. If you want past a barricade, you have got to dedicate yourself no matter the cost (risk) and without knowing the future (risk). With God all things are possible; with God I can do all things in Christ. When I am weak, He is strong.

A mindset that must be adopted as you launch yourself out of gridlock is that the God you and I serve is capable of both closing and opening doors. He is also able to redirect and correct my path if I by chance take off in the wrong direction. When I am tethered to the Father and engaged in a relationship with the Spirit, I am confident that any risk I take that is wrong, God can and will redirect. My prayer usually sounds something like, "Okay, God, to the best of my ability, this is the decision I think is right. If I am wrong, God, I give you full permission to derail this plan and open another door. I stay aware of your presence and promptings in this situation. AMEN."

Risk just means that what you are about to go for may or may not work. Some approaches do; some don't. But, every time you get a win out of the risk, you are *that much closer to your freedom*. And, every time you risk and it fails, you take all you learned in order to be *that much closer to your freedom*. Fear of failure is common. Fear of failure to the point of paraplegia is not. When paraplegia is your existence, it's coming from a place within that needs to get unraveled. Here is a giant bonus statement of truth: Usually, the risk that fails gets us further than the risk that's successful. *Failure has the ironic ability to lead to a higher rock than success does. Oh, and bonus statement of truth number two is: Our greatest success in the future is birthed out of our failures of the past, if we are living in the present!* You are welcome for the bonus statements, and you are now free to risk, risk, risk.

For the purposes of this book, it is important to know we must build grooves in the direction of and inside of the life model we want to exist within. We must have *dedication* to a particular way of doing life. A river runs where grooves have been worn down within the riverbed.

Right now, stop reading, close your eyes, and see a picture of that in your mind. See your energy carving out grooves by positive actions taken over and over and over. See the rushing waters tracing through the grooves you have worn, upstream and downstream. Deep thinking is actually the way our brains were made to learn, reverse toxic patterns, and grow new healthy ones. Deep thinking is also how our brains foster optimum health and learning ability. Our brains were not built to function chronically in short, starburst moments all day long. Ironically, this is the way our society and technology has forced us to exist. As I observe the lightning speed, rapid fire existence our teenagers live within 24/7 on Snapchat and other platforms, it is burdensome, to say the least. Without purposeful deep thinking on the right information, water pools up and becomes stagnant in areas that don't have a way out. Alternately, a whirlpool may build up in that area—in other words, a place that has blocked the water from following its natural path downstream.

Your mind has the deepest grooves where you have worn down the terrain by repeatedly visiting a particular state of mind. Whether dreading your fears or aligning with positive assessment, your brain now recalls those grooves in one thousandth of a second. When these grooves are built, the negative momentum shifts away. "But what if I am in lock down mode?" you ask. Then, you recite positive assessments in order to build the *certainty* muscle in your *mind first. The mind does not know the difference between thinking about something over and over and actually doing it.*

While in the hospital, I would stare at my running shoes sitting next to my bed and think deeply about all the times I had worn those shoes. I was building grooves in the lane I needed to stay within. I would imagine myself walking around Lady Bird Lake with Lauren or simply imagine being able to physically tend to Lauren when she needed me. Mind grooves lead to positive action.

The best example of building these mind grooves was my sessions on the ambulator. This was a state-of-the-art, hard-to-find machine resembling a treadmill, but with a body harness and leg casts. Anyone in a wheelchair, even a quadriplegic, could be strapped into the harness and leg casts. Once safely in place, the ambulator takes the patient through the motions of walking to reboot the mind, body, and nervous system connections. One of the special features of this machine is that it manages the amount of body weight that you actually place on the treadmill portion. That way, it can start simply by motion or by an actual grade of body weight. Although I was only able to start at maybe a ten percent of my body weight, the mind grooves it was building and accessing were impressive. It was building new grooves while accessing the positive memory I had stored from the times before. There was a full-length mirror in front of the ambulator, so I could connect brain to body to movement. This is done in the same way at physical therapy, if you want your right leg to do something that it cannot do—you have your brain focus on the left leg doing it over and over. I continue to use this theory today with great success in my physical therapy sessions.

You can begin to build mind grooves that eventually manifest action! Eventually, the grooves begin to shift your life from fear to faith, from lies to truth, from lockdown to freedom. I can tell you with one thousand percent certainty that I built grooves while in the hospital out of a belief system that created momentum that said, "I will run again—this is going to work! I was made to move, and I will move. Oh, and by the way, God is carrying me." This mindset was coupled with deep thinking as I attempted to put action within the mental grooves. In tandem, new belief systems and dedication will build momentum and have a compound effect on your life.

You can think of it also in terms of your faith. There is a similar behavior that takes place when we obey scripture. The renewing of the mind creates the same effect in our lives by building spiritual grooves. There is a reason we are instructed to meditate on it day and night. Are you stuck, unsure of your next move? Roman 12:2 (NIV) says, "Do not conform to the pattern of this world but be transformed by the renewing of your mind. Then you will be able to test and approve what God's will is—his good, pleasing and perfect will." The Message translation reads, "Don't become so well-adjusted to your culture that you fit into it without even thinking. Instead, fix your attention on God. You'll be changed from the inside out. Readily recognize what he wants from you, and quickly respond to it. Unlike the culture around you, always dragging you down to its level of immaturity, God brings the best out of you, develops well-formed maturity [grooves] in you." Wow, so good. We need new *mind* grooves.

Are you missing spiritual grooves? If so, your spiritual river has water backed up either into whirlpools that go nowhere or into cesspools that are stagnant. As believers, we know that the Holy Spirit in our lives produces rivers of flowing water coming from deep within us. These free-flowing rivers bring clarity, awareness, and motivation to get us out of lockdown. They are accessible at *all* times. Little by little, as we access the power of the Holy Spirit through the Word and prayer, spiritual grooves are built that allow this water to flow freely throughout our lives. The groove concept works for every area of our lives.

In my business life, there was once a client I really wanted to work with. Initially, I was petrified to call on them and could not figure out what it was about them that had me roadblocked. I began to form well-worn grooves in my mind about what the perfect outcome could be. I rehearsed it over and over. I rehearsed objections and the positive outcome I desired until, one day, a mind shift happened. I called on the person in charge, he threw objections my way, and we negotiated. I left with one of our company's biggest advertisers, who later became a good friend and one of our company's advocates.

I have spoken about hunger having been the driving and sustaining factor when it came to walking out of my wheelchair for those twelve years. Then, just recently, I came across the subject in a marketing program I was being trained in by Tony Robbins and Dean Graziosi. These guys are mega successful and have sixty years of combined intelligence in the world of studying what makes people succeed or fail. They said, "The common denominator of ALL successful people in the world" is HUNGER. Many of the stories throughout the ages are of men and women who, because of some sort of lockdown mode or from places of being stuck, used hunger to regain their mobility. Hunger helped them to rise out of paralysis into the lives we study to this day in business and in life (which are one and the same when I am teaching).

Hunger! A drive that never goes away and creates a willingness to keep going. Someone who will not settle for less than they can be has hunger. The beautiful thing about you and me and everyone else reading this book is that we can all find this place within us. Hunger pushes down barriers so we can truly live. And truly living does not involve lockdown and stuck-ed-ness.

Hunger separates the dabblers from the warriors.

Here is a little of what dedication looked like as I entered the rehab hospital. There were three aspects of dedication at work. One, I was literally obsessed with the outcome. This level of dedication was releasing an energy that allowed me to find answers. Something super cool was also happening, and it will happen for you too: a God-created innate process occurred in the Reticular Activating System (RAS) of my brain. The RAS is a bundle of nerves at our brainstem that filters out unnecessary information so that the important stuff gets through. Your RAS takes what you focus on and creates a filter for it. It then sifts through the data you encounter daily and presents only the pieces that are important to you. You then begin to see *more of what you have purposed your mind, will, and emotions on*.

For instance, have you ever chosen a baby name and then, seemingly all of a sudden, everywhere you go that name appears? Or, how about a car? You research and long over a particular type vehicle, and then you see it everywhere you go! If you have more fear stored than freedom, your mind will find fear. If you have more lies stored than truth, your mind will seek information that agrees with the lies. And, if you purpose yourself on hope, you will begin to see it everywhere! That is the RAS at work.

This system is one of the reasons you and I can have the stamina necessary to build hunger and put down deep roots of dedication. On the flip side, if you have a limiting belief system that everyone is out to get you, you are scared, everyone has it better than you do, or you get passed over every single time, *that* is all you will see!

The second aspect of dedication at work was, I began to take unrelenting massive action. This looked like "inch, adjust, inch, adjust" and so on.

The third aspect was ridiculously fierce focus on what I wanted, not what I didn't want. Are you starting to see that your job is engaging in the hard work of *repetition*? And, remembering the fact that God is carrying you! Press in, press in, press in with energy guided in the direction you established in the phases of decision and declaration.

The brain has to be properly engaged. The idea that you have to actively maneuver your own brain creates a mind explosion for many people. The majority of society operates as puppets to whatever their brain throws their way. A paralyzing statement gets birthed that says, "This is just the way I am!" and that statement has to be dealt with. Every single reality starts with a thought.

I want to share something with you that will be instrumental in your success. It is the basic understanding of one of the driving forces behind why we stay dedicated to something and see it through. Lucky for you, I am a brain science geek. And hunger, passion, and commitment require a well-functioning brain system. The exercise that I'm about to walk you through could very well immediately answer the question about why you do or do not stay on course. The issue could very well be the paralyzing cycle going on in your brain.

Picture this...

Every thought that enters our mind is tangible and trackable. Every thought has an emotion, and that emotion is where our behavior stems. Take a look at your emotional state. It will

tell you what you are thinking and confirm why you are an emotional mess or an emotional powerhouse. Out of that emotion
comes our attitude. Take it one step further, and we now have
every thought tied to an emotion and every emotion not only
creating a behavior but creating a behavior with a chemical reaction attached to it! That chemical reaction courses through
the body and, depending on the initial thought that we allow, it
produces either positive endorphins creating positive energy
and confidence, or anxiety or depression and sickness. And the
kicker: it is all stored for further recall. Hence, the buzz word
"trigger" was born. Hello, trigger!

Human emotion, not human knowledge, fuels action when
viewed in this manner. That is why you can *know* a lot yet not
have many results. Maybe today you are reading this thinking, "I
know 'it,' but I cannot get myself out of this state of paraplegia."
That feeling is common, and the good news is that we *all* have
the capacity to direct or redirect, and thereby change, emotion.
Just as we *all* have the same access to the spirit of God. The
problem that leads to knowing but not accomplishing is, we are
not emotionally fit. We have been jerked around for so long
from skewed thought syndromes and belief systems (and we've
ALLOWED IT) that we are never in a state of readiness to take
authority. *We have to **pursue** positive emotion.* Remember
those grooves we just talked about? The same principle applies
here. I have heard great leaders say that having emotion is not
the same as having emotional intelligence. Emotions can become a habit. Let me say that again: *emotions can become a
habit.*

Hunger cannot thrive in an environment (or brain) that is
vacillating back and forth. Think alignment! We have to train our
brains to stop negotiating with ourselves. Train your brain to

think, "This is how I operate! In faith, decisively!" We have to stop "shoulding" all over ourselves. Stop betraying our own selves. *Momentum is non-existent in the midst of self-betrayal.* Betrayal is a deep infraction that humans do unto each other that takes decades to be healed from (if it ever happens at all). Yet, we betray our own selves multiple times a day as we go back on what we said we were dedicated to accomplishing.

I have betrayed myself in so many different seasons out of fear that people might not like me or might not think I'm good enough or that I've made too many mistakes. Honestly, the horrible habit of betraying ourselves happens countless times a day and is almost ingrained to the point of no return. Let's look at just a few: not turning off the television and working out, hitting the snooze button over and over, never getting around to earning that certificate that would make you more promotable, taking that toxic phone call once again, making that toxic phone call once again, walking past your Bible and instead engaging in a mindless habit that keeps you feeling guilty. Are you starting to get the picture? If you feel down and low on energy, stop betraying yourself. Are you starting to see that maybe even you have a thread of "shoulding on yourself" syndrome?

More often, though, my own self-betrayal has stemmed from poor brain health (that I allowed) and, in turn, it produced depression that caused me to continue to abandon myself. Through personal growth, I have also become aware that the more solid I get in my faith and the greater understanding I gain of my identity, the more I respect myself and, hence, the less betrayal I engage in. You are worth self-respect! Logically, this repetitive self-betrayal makes no sense, and yet we let these limits dictate our life's outcome. Self-betrayal sabotages this critical element of dedication to our ultimate mobility. Please let me save you precious time and money. Stop betraying yourself. It does require discipline that isn't always comfortable, but the latter is not an option any longer. You are coming out of lock-down! The truer you are to yourself, the more impactful you become. If you cannot get yourself out of this cycle, allow me to help you unravel the cord that is keeping you locked down. The freedom from this *one* thing will unleash hunger like nothing else in your life. I will let you in on a little secret: Reversing this process of self-betrayal depends upon recognizing your personal value and your clearly defined life values. It is more than likely a belief buried layers deep, but it is able to be unearthed and re-versed!

We are heading towards the end of the conversation on what happened in that moment in the ICU when I souled out to decision, declaration, and dedication. Maybe, even after all this insight, you are thinking, "I've already tried all of this." Trying is not enough! This is *dedication* we are talking about. Trying means half-heartedly giving it a whirl while your mindset is har-boring a belief that it probably isn't going to work. We can claim dedication to something and still not get the results we desire. Is it plausible that you *have* indeed tried, but you've done so with only a portion of your potential capability due to a skewed belief system? Much of our problem comes from the need for brain training and the building of mind grooves.

That is exactly what happened to me for years in the course of "trying" to write this book. Before I tell you the story, let me make clear that I wholeheartedly believe in divine timing for certain things to occur. That truth is part of my book writing story, but it can also be used as an excuse or crutch as a way out of finally attaining your next level. My book writing problem was way more about a habit problem, and you might have the same issue in your own life.

For about ten years, I longed to write this book. Time upon frustrating time, I "tried" to get it done. Many times, I would get knocked off course by my mind telling me that my story really didn't matter. In earlier years, I did not have adequate brain retraining like I have now. When focus got tough or life intervened, that self-limiting mind story subconsciously allowed me to set the work aside. For the life of me I could not figure out why this girl who majored in journalism could not complete a book about a story she had lived! Over and over, I purposed to write, and I'd write, write, and write some more. There was no plan in place; I'd just write here and there, now and then. Honestly, I eventually felt paralyzed after several years circling around the same mountain. I wanted it, I longed for it, I could see it. But one major thing was missing: habit.

There was no scheduled plan on the actual day-to-day calendar I lived by. I had goals. I've always been a goal setter. But goals are not habits. This entire epiphany played out on my podcast, L!ve with Amy, dated January 2 and 14, 2020. I encourage you to listen to these podcasts; they got rave reviews!

My teenage daughter approached me towards the end of 2019 and said, "Mom let's do our vision boards for next year." The happiest mom alive, I of course agreed. I had been a goal-setter during my thirty-five years as a sales and marketing executive and had reached many of the goals I set for myself. There were also many I had missed the mark on. Lauren and I began our boards and I was trying to cheat off of hers (it was super creative). I realized my board was missing a key ingredient to success: habits. I got another poster board and started over. My board became one of habits that I would schedule and implement with the help of an accountability coach. I had a manuscript ready for first edit five months later! Habits and accountability *must* exist and be scheduled in order for you to remain dedicated.

We have unconscious beliefs about everything in life that either benefit us or betray us. What is needed is the kind of discovery work that I provide in The Freedom Success Method™—the kind that uncovers what is keeping you roadblocked. Once discovered, you can begin birthing the desired results for your next-level life such as reinventing yourself, believing you are C-Suite material, or launching that company or product. This is done in our mind first, over and over and over, with enough repetition to etch out "belief grooves." It is not exhausting, it is natural. Through the grooves your vision begins to flow like a river. Then, you begin to take massive, dedicated action.

Repetition is the mother of all skill. You have to stop dabbling in order to get out of lockdown. Half-hearted was not an option for me as I headed out of the ICU to Health South Hospital and towards the next twelve years of my mobility life, and it is not an option for you. You have to decide you are *all in*—in other words, *dedicated*.

Throughout my years in ministry I have worked with women who were frustrated with God and frustrated with faith. After discovery, it was evident that their failing model had been one of "one foot in and one foot out." Their declaration was not aligning with their dedication. That misalignment causes an insurmountable barrier! A double-minded woman is unstable in all her ways.

Of course new action has to happen and work has to be done, but that work does not include more beating up of oneself or fleeing (going into fight-or-flight mode). Both reactions are exhausting. This work is mind work, will work, and spirit work. You've got to sit with it, shushing the hell out of the outside world (literally) and the battle within! Sitting with your maker, renewing your mind, and aligning your will. Listen to that still soft voice inside that is revealing and ready to be aligned. If all the Bible is true, and I choose to believe that it is, then He meant it when he said "...come to me all you who are weary and I will give you rest... I will reveal things to you that you do not know." Our faith walk is a perfect example of how soul-dedication (mind, will, and emotions) fosters an all-consuming hunger.

Here is another secret: During this process, you use energy not force. I will focus on this statement throughout the book for all of you super exhausted, worn-out souls. I *was* you! When I grasped the concept of energy, not force, results came faster and more smoothly, and I sustained the energy necessary to finish the task at hand. The other factor is that you have far more energy than you think you do in order to walk out of the wheelchair that life has placed you in. Your problem is that your energy is dedicated to the wrong things. When we become paralyzed or stuck, we have experienced negative energy momentum to the point of paralysis.

What are you dedicated to? What takes precedence in your life no matter what? If we assessed your life, would it look, smell, and taste the way you claim that it does? Is it representative of the wants, needs, desires, and longings of your heart? I created an exercise to assess the sobering truth related to this assessment. It involves uncovering what you say you firmly believe, after which point an assessment is done within each pertinent area of your life and with regard to different behaviors within those categories. People are shocked to discover that what they say they believe or are dedicated to is vastly out of alignment when compared to their day-to-day lives. Not too long ago, I took myself through this exercise. I was overwhelmed with a misalignment I observed in my own life, even as someone who focuses on this stuff all the time! I quickly took myself through the re-alignment process.

I heard it once said that the most important person to learn from is yourself. Through my journey out of paralysis, I have found that to be true. Let me explain a bit. Most of us haven't a clue what is going on deep within. Going through the *discovery* process as an *observer* is enlightening and life-altering. Again, use energy, not force. You can have all the skill, tactics, and talent of anyone in the world and still not be able to get yourself out of lockdown or across a barricade because of mindset and emotions. More times than not, we are fighting the wrong problem! That is exactly why I developed The Freedom Success Method™. To walk people out of this syndrome once and for all.

Let's go a bit deeper into my journey finding my way out of paralysis. Warning: The next chapter will rock your world of perspective. Perspective is a serious game-changer and if not grasped, you will stay stuck in lockdown.

PERSPECTIVE

I was transferred out of the ICU by ambulance to Health South Hospital, where I spent the next couple of months, from sun-up to sun-down, involved with rehab and nursing care. The paramedics delivered me to the floor I would reside on. As they pushed my gurney around the hallway to the nurses' station, I heard one of the nurses refer to me as a "para" (paraplegic). She said, "The para we are waiting for just arrived." Hearing that nurse refer to me as a "para" sent me to an emotional abyss I had never before known—a deep dark place with myself, my condition, and my God. That night, as I pulled the covers over my head, reality was sinking further and further in. It was the closest I'd ever been to the face of my maker.

Certainly, I had cried out many times before, but none of them compared to this. Bruised, battered, and oppressed after my first marriage ended, I cried out. As a young woman lost in a seemingly hopeless cycle of anxiety, drugs and alcohol, I cried out. Now, here in the cold, stale, hospital room, I cried out. This time, however, was different because of the depth of loss at hand.

The Lord showed up in that room and spoke to the depths of my grief. What I heard that night was God's wisdom speaking to me. It wasn't an audible voice but instead simply thoughts that were clearly not my own. What I heard was, "Amy, move forward as if you are birthing something and not as if you have been stolen from." Profound wisdom visited me. "Move forward as if you are birthing something and not as if you have been stolen from."

Think of this in terms of your own situation. Birthing something holds so much expectation and anticipation. There is opportunity and new life when birthing something. Being stolen from, on the other hand, makes us feel cheated, robbed, invaded, angry, and less than. I knew in that moment God had just given me a universal message—and it wasn't just for me then; it's also for you as you read this book. When wisdom visits you, it will change the trajectory of your life if you act on it.

Some of you have been stolen from, robbed, and cheated, but the ball is in your court in terms of what you do with that. Will you birth something from it or live your life broken, bitter, angry, and sad? I moved forward with this wisdom and began to take back what had been stolen as if I was birthing something beautiful, powerful, and determined. *My perspective was radically redirected that night.*

Where we see death, there can be life. We have to want to see it (perspective). It might take time, but that is part of the healing process. Sometimes after trauma or tragedy we do not want to see the light or life. We need to be in the dark. But at some point, we are meant to emerge out of ashes. We are not meant to deteriorate. There is a time for everything under the sun, a time to rejoice and a time to mourn. Allow yourself to experience the darkness, but not for longer than is needed or else the darkness will blind you to the light of perspective.

I have benefited from and love to teach the process of find it, feel it, express it and heal it. It is an incredibly effective tool. The order is of importance and I can teach you how.

There are few things more important for success than having the right mental set point, the right perspective. People fail horribly because they are looking at obstacles, injustice, pain, and loss. How long are you going to allow your life to be stolen? Genuinely ask yourself this question: Why am I allowing this situation to rob me day-in and day-out? Do I believe I have a choice? Sit with the questions. Questions often dismantle confusion and loosen the vice grip we have on a particular set point that does not serve us well any longer. And, as a side thought, as I write this there is social injustice occurring and reactions to it that fall perfectly in line with this conversation. If you are allowing a situation to remain in order to get even, remain in control, or try and make the past better, it is time for a birth. None of those desired outcomes will ever propel you anywhere positive. Staring at the injustice keeps the shackles locked.

I am aware that it can feel like you cannot release the darkness, but I am here to tell you that you are the *only* one who can. A stolen-from perspective says, "I've locked myself into a losing mindset, waiting for the darkness to heal and release me." That is a lie. And, while it's completely illogical, we often return to or remain in darkness, expecting to get our answers or healing or justice from that place of infraction. There are lessons to be learned from the past, but I have honestly learned those lessons in moving forward toward a solution. A visual example is, I am in the grocery store pushing my cart one direction while looking down an opposite isle. It rarely ends well! Needing to learn to walk again while looking back at a blunder will only keep you stuck. I urge you, in that dark space, to do something new that might open a door that shifts your perspective.

I often tell the redemptive story of how I left home a broken young woman to start my adult life aspiring to the level at which I viewed myself. Honestly, that level was not very high. Subconsciously, because of what others had done to me and what I had done to myself, I set a pretty low standard for myself. It caused such low self-esteem. And, a recurring theme in those earlier years was how esteemed my life looked on the outside while I felt dismantled on the inside. After many years of failed attempts to shake the lowliness off of my life, I began to see possibility through other people's lives. I began to ask, "Why not me?" I could absolutely do what others were doing. The perspective (mindset) I had about my life shifted as I opened my heart to the possibility presented in asking, "Why not me?" Let me tell you, from that point, things started to fall in line. Healthy relationships showed up, I had the courage to get rid of toxic relationships, I stepped up my spiritual game, and I doubled my income. I rid myself of everything that reminded me of the disgusting, false perspective that I accepted in a state of emotional paralysis. The plasticity of the brain was at work, shifting and reshaping. Be aware that in a state of trauma or crisis, we adopt perspectives that follow us through life long past their time. Never ever let the voice of scoffers set you back. For years, as my standards were being raised, scoffers hurt my heart. But now I am free from that. Truly living free is living free of your "scoffers." Set that new standard and stop apologizing for it!

One small shift of your face in a different direction is all it takes. Remember, renewed perspective arrives through energy, not force. It arrives as you are moving through the darkness, but you must allow yourself, give yourself permission, to walk again. There is ALWAYS a solution for unresolved pain that is keeping us from our next-level life. However, what is in the dark must be brought to light in order to be resolved. Your next-level life is a John 10:10 life. A life to the fullest.

Perspective rigidity will keep you in lockdown. Allowing your perspective to be blown by the wind also creates a roadblock by way of putting you in a spin cycle. I am not suggesting that a total overhaul of perspective is needed every time and every place that you feel stuck. I am, however, suggesting that if you do not become a person *willing* to consider new or even different ideas of how to look at your situation, you will stay right where you are, stale and frustrated. What I am bringing to light is this: When we have eyes to see but do not see, and when we have ears to hear but do not hear, we will stay in perspective paralysis.

One of the hardest things in the world to do is to agree that there is a different way to see something from the way you have seen it for a very long time, especially when trauma is involved. If you want to rid your mind, will, or emotions of paralysis, you will have to make a shift in your perspective. Why is it so difficult to make this shift? First and foremost, pride. Next, if your perspective was formed out of hurt, betrayal, loss, or pain, there is a huge chance that your perspective—although it seems to be your reality—may be skewed and lodged in your subconscious.

Type-A personalities (strong-willed go-getters), I am talking to you because I *am* you. If you cannot imagine that someone younger or older in your industry might have a way of doing things that makes more sense, you cannot—you will not—reach your next-level life. I experienced this first-hand when I was working with the number-one radio group in our city. I was promoted to Business Development Director and had the daunting task of introducing a new way of selling radio to over twenty-five seasoned, successful, and mostly Type-A sales executives. It just so happened that I was willing to adopt this non-traditional way of selling radio and had astronomical success with it. All parties involved knew this to be true. Even though this opportunity would put more money into their pockets and lead to greater overall success, their perspective of how to sell radio was nearly impenetrable. It would involve a learning curve, creativity, and a bit more time investment, but the end result was gold. Plain and simple, sometimes we refuse perspective redirection out of stubbornness, a crappy attitude, ego, or fear even when the end result is almost certain gold. Quite simply, if you want to achieve the next level, you have to be willing to open yourself to a new perspective.

Another person who helps teach me how to embrace different viewpoints (or balance the one I have) is my teenage daughter. I don't always agree with her, but I stop and consider whether or not what she is saying might call for a perspective shift on my part. Learning and considering another generation's perspective can be fascinating, and it's imperative to business success as well as parenting.

Another great example from one of the planet's best therapists was learned during a counseling session with my spouse. The therapist taught me to sit with responses that I wholeheartedly disagreed with (which was super irritating at first), in the mind space of "This is the other person's experience, whether or not it is mine." Giving pause to someone else's "experience"—one that was polar opposite my own—gave me a moment to shift, pick up a new lens, and consider the possibilities. Sometimes my perspective remained, and sometimes just the tiniest shift from that exercise brought peace, understanding, and revelation.

The other best therapist on the planet is my friend Tracey Brock. She was a guest on my radio program, L!ve with Amy, and in our conversation she said something that made me stop dead in my tracks. She said to the listeners, *"How do other people experience you? What do others encounter on the other side of you?"* Now that is a question! Considering that question thoughtfully in and of itself just might change your perspective about a particular situation in any of your relationships. This is beyond worth stopping and pondering. Consider any of your relationships: kids, spouse, boss, service staff, volunteer acquaintances, or neighbors—all the different people and groups that you encounter within the week. What do they see of you from their side? Be honest with yourself, and provide no justifications or "That is just the way I am" statements. This conversation is between you and you! I'm encouraging you to have it because, when I took myself through this exercise, it shifted my perspective and caused me to adjust some of my behavior. When we can appreciate two varying degrees of perspective, take the best from both and carry on, we become free.

No human being wants to let go of what they are certain is the right perspective. We refuse out of pride, both at home and in the workplace. We refuse out of prejudice, and we refuse out of bullheadedness. This can make you a very difficult and unpleasant person to be around. Nobody likes someone who is always right and rigid. Are you like this? Be honest with yourself.

There is a large chance that even when you open yourself up to a different perspective, you will indeed remain true to your original mindset. There is also a large chance that you will open up your mind to alternate paths that will lead to a new perspective. From this willingness to be curious, you might find your way out and be astonished that you didn't see this other perspective sooner. We have to be willing to hear people with varying viewpoints, different generations, different ethnicities that see life through totally different lenses. And, depending on the past we have endured, if we *don't* open our minds, look up, let go, and let God, we will likely die with many gifts still inside of us and many opportunities lost. Many dreams will go unlived, and we will live out the one and only life we get as a prisoner. Perspective rigidity is prison. Nobody wants that.

Another huge consideration is not so much with regard to exactly what our perspective is but also where it is coming from. Build an awareness of what movie reel your brain is cycling. I'm not referring to thoughts directly on the surface. Go a level deeper. That is the reel that is keeping you paralyzed from your next-level life. This is your subconscious mind, and you get the chance, at any given time, to make new decisions regarding data you input long ago. Remember, implement kindergarten-level instructions with college-level discipline. Doing this requires maturity. You have to pause and peel back another layer of the metaphorical onion. If your viewpoint has you stuck, you *must* examine where it came from in the first place. Look, we don't know what we don't know. We also don't know what we've never paused and thought about, hence the phrases, "Wow, I've never thought about that" and "Wow, I never saw it like that."

Two things are going to be discovered beneath this top layer. One, you have likely literally never thought about things this deeply, so you must commit to considering openly, learning, and moving forward. The other discovery, depending on how honest you're willing to be, will be the awareness of a perspective formed during a time in your life when there was major misalignment of your soul. You might discover a perspective lodged from negativity that formed a belief that does not align with who you are or want to become. Many times, these disserving beliefs innocently enough come from our caregivers, extended family members, coaches, educators, and even spiritual authorities.

One of the mottos I live by says, "If you don't stand for something, you will fall for anything." Perspective shift is not always about going in a totally different direction from your original stance. Many times, it is about shifting, considering, gaining, combining with your current perspective (or not), and moving to a higher plain. Does that make sense? My desire is to support you as you emerge from lockdown based on a perspective that has failed to get you to your next level.

The bottom line is, if you didn't need a perspective redirection, you would already be where you desire to go.

Allow God to bring a perspective redirect into your life. There is not a single soul exempt from needing a perspective shift or overhaul at a point, if not many points, of life!

The following story is very difficult to tell, but if my precious friend can allow for a perspective redirection within her experience, so can you and I. My friend has lived through an unimaginable tragedy. She was involved in the co-sleeping death of her child, who was only a few months old. She is an amazing woman, and she is growing through her story. But, like many of us, it was not her first rodeo with unexpected outcomes. She was already living through the fallout of a dysfunctional and broken childhood home and did not yet have her demons silenced.

She shared this statement with me, and I want you to think deeply about it: "I have heard people talk about the fact that they do not know if they have the kind of faith that can bring them through a major trial or not. The only thing I can think when I hear that is, 'Unfortunately, the only way you can know WITHOUT A DOUBT is to go through the worst hell of your life.' *Have faith before the hell!* Be grateful if it hasn't been tested. And, if it has been tested, be grateful that you still have faith. *God doesn't change* where He is before or after a trial; the only thing that changes is our perspective. And, *perspective is 100 percent of life.* There is no such thing as rock bottom until you're dead. Rock bottom is where you decide it is. It can AL-WAYS get worse. No matter how bad it is, you can be grateful it isn't worse." That same woman believes that child's purpose in life was to be the catalyst she needed to make some specific life changes. She is convinced that those changes would have come no other way, instead leaving her in bondage, living and loving at only half her capacity to do either!

Perspective. My friend has learned that even in death there can be a re-birth. This woman has chosen the perspective that God was with her before, during, and after her tragedy. She has chosen to see that she became a different woman from that incident, a woman who serves the children she still has.

If you are a person of faith, you know that God speaks to the details of our lives through the details of the characters within the Bible. Consider these stories in relation to your perspective journey.

Moses was the greatest Jewish leader and set the Exodus in motion to save the Israelite people. Look at the perspective Moses had about himself versus God's perspective.

MOSES' PERSPECTIVE

Moses said to the Lord, "Pardon your servant, Lord. I have never been eloquent, neither in the past nor since you have spoken to your servant. I am slow of speech and tongue." Moses was saying, "I can't speak, never have spoken, don't know how, and am really uncomfortable with it."

GOD'S PERSPECTIVE

The Lord said to him, "Who gave human beings their mouths? Who makes them deaf or mute? Who gives them sight or makes them blind? Is it not I, the Lord? Now go; I will help you speak and will teach you what to say." In other words, "I made you and your mouth, so why wouldn't I help you make it work properly? Plus, I have every power under the sun. I've got this. Just say yes."

Another Biblical example of perspective is when David, the lowly shepherd small in frame, boldly kills a fierce giant of a man. The people surrounding David had their perspective of the situation, and David had his. They were diabolically different.

THE PEOPLE'S PERSPECTIVE

"You can't go and fight this Philistine. You're too young and inexperienced—and he's been at this fighting business since before you were born." 1 Samuel 17:33

DAVID'S PERSPECTIVE

Hey, I've killed a lion and a bear; this Philistine is nothing. "The Lord who delivered me from the paw of the lion and the paw of the bear will deliver me from the hand of this Philistine (Goliath). 1 Samuel 17: 37

In both these examples, Moses and David shifted their perspectives and were willing to see into a situation differently. This led to astounding results. Just like the wisdom imparted to me as I lied in my bed that first night at the rehab center, I could have shifted perspective and seen with new eyes that produced astounding results—or I could have *not* shifted and become an angry, bitter, non-walking woman who blamed God and everybody else for the loss of my mobility.

I fought the battle from a place of being committed to birthing something, not from a lack mindset. My resolve has been to birth, for twelve years, week after week after week in faith.

FAITH, FACTS, AND A MIRACLE

The facts said I was destined for blood clots. The facts said I would have to self-catheterize. The facts said it would be a miracle to fully recover. The spinal cord is the control tower of the body. It communicates with the brain to signal muscles, nerves, and organs to perform their assigned functions. The cord is made up of an integral network of nerves that runs from the brain to the lower body. This nerve network controls every system in the human body. Even minimal disruption to the network can have lasting, catastrophic results to our body's function. The big question leaving the ICU and transferring to the rehab hospital was, *Will I move forward on facts or faith?* The facts did not consider miracles, nor did they consider my faith. The facts did not take into consideration what I was about to discover had transpired while I was on the surgical table.

She came through the door with a huge grin on her face, blonde ringlets bouncing around her face, and a little shimmy in her step.

"Surprise, Mommy!" Greg kept Lauren home from Pre-K that day so that they could both bring me home. Leaving this safe environment frightened me. The care was there, the schedule worked, and I knew that without them I would be forced to move into uncharted territory. It was time to embark on the next dimension of this journey and gain more independence and more strength through an outpatient program. We packed up my belongings and were off to a long-awaited appointment with my neurosurgeon, Dr. Kemper.

I had not seen him since the day the ambulance arrived to transport me to Health South Rehab Hospital. Finally, we would discuss the details of the previous surgery and get his opinion about what was already being called a miracle by my rehab doctor, therapists, and nurses.

Entering surgery, we were aware I had developed a condition called hydromyelia. This condition forms a hole or sack where the tumor resides, a hole that fills with fluid. It is very difficult for that space to close and heal, and if it doesn't it wreaks more havoc in the cord, possibly needing a shunt or tube to redirect fluid, which can seriously affect motor and sensory function. My motor skills were already shot. During surgery, I also lost sensory to hot, cold, and sharp sensations in my trunk and down my left side to my toes. That remains the case to this day. Dr. Kemper had already warned that continued hydromyelia was not a situation we wanted to be in, but it was a real possibility.

I arrived at the appointment in horrible pain but set it aside temporarily to ensure that I took in every word he had to say. He examined me and had nothing but sheer joy in his countenance (as much as a neurosurgeon can express). We discussed the rupturing effect the tumor presented and how difficult it was for him to determine the difference between cord and tumor. I asked him about the size of the tumor, and he replied, 'It's about the size of a grape." He reminded us that the edge of the cord where the tumor had hemorrhaged was the thickness of a piece of paper. Had the tumor crossed through that barrier, there would have been no opportunity for recovery. Timing was everything!

Just as we were about to leave, he added as an afterthought, "Oh, by the way, as I removed the bulk of the tumor, that hole from hydromyelia closed shut right before our eyes. We have never seen that before! It was amazing." My miracle. The ability to heal was given to me that day on the surgical table. God had worked on my behalf, and I did not even know it.

He is working on your behalf right now! Do you feel like you are being chiseled and cut on and dissected on a surgical table? Do you feel like you have lost your mobility? Do you feel paralyzed? The spirit of the living God is working on your behalf. It is not about how you feel; it is about what you believe. Do you believe in the miracle of a resurrected God who has imparted His spirit into you and who can perform a miracle in your life? Faith believes in the impossible. I have a plaque in my home that says, "Faith does not make things happen; it makes them possible."

Faith not facts is exactly how Roger Banister did something no one else had ever done. In fact, the word on the street was that breaking a four-minute mile was humanly impossible. In 1954, at the age of twenty-five, Roger Bannister made headlines around the world as the first person to run a mile under four minutes. Bannister's 3:59:04 mile unlocked the door to what was possible in track, both physically and psychologically. Once Banister broke the record, it began being broken all across the world. The "fact barrier" had been removed. According to Wikipedia, that barrier has been broken by over 1,400 men and is now the gold standard for the race. Bannister said he wanted his record not only to be remembered in sports *but also as we seek what seems to be unachievable in life.*

My Roger Bannister story began the evening the ambulance arrived at the rehab hospital and nurses began to arrive and introduce themselves. One in particular stood out. He greeted me and was extremely friendly, wanting to know my story and what had happened. After I finished talking, he began to give his assessment of what was about to occur there in the hospital. As we addressed my catheter and the fact that it was going to stay in for a while, he *confirmed* that I would get bladder infections because of the length of time the catheter would be in place. He also confirmed that more than likely I would have to self-catharize once it was removed.

"Everyone gets bladder infections." As the last syllable hit his lips, I said, "In Jesus' holy name! I will not have to self-catharize in order to urinate nor will I get an infection!" They would need to put me to sleep to make that happen. Some of you may have a fear of flying or perhaps of needles, snakes, or the dentist. I had a fear of self-catharization!

What do faith, facts, and catharization have to do with each other? Let me make the connection for you. Having someone else catheterize me was loathsome, but the idea of doing it myself was worse, and it was *not* an option. As happy as I was about the day arriving for the catheter removal, the follow-up procedure to ensure I could urinate on my own had me in anxiety and fear. My rehab doctor had also carefully explained the "facts." She basically said that when the catheter comes out, *no one—or very few, if any—ever* do not have to self-catheterize to get their bladder working. Literally losing sleep over this possibility, I had already called my friend Krissy to describe the hell I was possibly facing. I said, "You have got to pray, Krissy!"

All day long I prayed. I was convinced they would have to sedate me to be catheterized again, which they of course weren't going to agree to do. I enlisted every nurse's and technician's ear that passed by in a desperate attempt to hear something that would calm my panic. It never happened. Each only smiled and said that everyone who was paralyzed went through it. No one urinates right off the bat, they assured me, all the while I was thinking, "In the holy name of God, I will pee!" They had not yet met my overactive bladder. She had lived with me for a very long while. I did not count on her failing me now! I came in with an overactive bladder, and by gosh I planned on leaving with an overactive bladder.

Maybe an hour passed after the catheter came out. I peed! Boldly pressing the call button, I announced to the nurses' station that I'd had success. But, an ultrasound had to be conducted to ensure the bladder had fully emptied. Hearing that ultrasound cart come down the hallway quickly became a sound I hated. In walked Debra, who had become one of several favorite nurses. Ultrasound in hand, she was ready. Firmly rubbing the wand on my belly, the cc's measured were not enough.

Well aware that I was emotionally distraught and knowing I had been praying audibly in my room about this situation, she smiled as she said I was a few cc's short. Self-catheterization was looming, and I instructed her to leave the room. "I can pee on command! Give me five minutes." Hallelujah, I peed. I press the call button for Debra. I was shouting joyously, she was laughing, and I was repeating, "Thank you, thank you, thank you." By this point, the nurses knew where my help came from!

This process went on for well over a week to ensure all systems were go *and not once did I have to self-catheterize!* Just call me Amy Banister! *Faith and not facts.*

It's a bit of a rocky segue from catharizing to a spiritual reference from ancient script on this subject. But let's go for it.

Facts were that Goliath was a giant of a man. He was angry, huge, and crazy strong. David was small and not trained. He was not a warrior by nature. What David had was faith and a fighting spirit, and he defeated the giant. Factually, Shadrach, Meshach, and Abednego were tossed into the fire. Faith was the protection they held onto that allowed them to overcome the reality of the heat. They left the incinerator without even smelling of smoke. (#firegoals)

Lastly, Daniel did, in fact, get tossed in with the lion. He had radical faith (much like mine when it came to urination) that God would deliver him. That lion's mouth was closed shut. *People who defy the odds believe that they can, and their faith moves mountains*!

Faith is *confidence* in what we hope for and *assurance* of what we do not see. This is a quality for which the ancients were commended. By faith we understand that the universe was formed at God's command so that what is seen was not made out of what was visible. Hebrews 11:1-3 (NIV)

For us to clearly understand that faith is not complete without action, I'll let James say it better than I ever could:

James 2:14-26: What good is it, my brothers and sisters, if someone claims to have faith but has no deeds? Can such faith save them? Suppose a brother or a sister is without clothes and daily food. If one of you says to them, "Go in peace; keep warm and well fed," but does nothing about their physical needs, what good is it? In the same way, faith by itself, if it is not accompanied by action, is dead.

But someone will say, "You have faith; I have deeds."

Show me your faith without deeds, and I will show you my faith by my deeds. You believe that there is one God. Good! Even the demons believe that—and shudder.

You foolish person, do you want evidence that faith without deeds is useless?... You see that a person is considered righteous by what they do and not by faith alone... As the body without the spirit is dead, so faith without deeds is dead.

Life gets very exciting and possibility becomes endless when we refuse the lies of logic. Living with faith in action produces results. I am here to testify that not only did I not have to self-catheterize, I did not get blood clots, my bowels regained their function, and I walked out of my wheelchair!

Faith is much like a perspective redirect. Faith sends us in the direction we want to go before any substantive proof arrives. While operating in faith, my countenance is uplifted and the things I need for success fall in place more easily. Right faith equals right mindset equals right perspective equals brain reaction equals emotion equals chemical reaction equals desired result!

For most of my life, especially in business, I've chosen to live a "What if" existence. Not the kind you are perhaps thinking about. Not a life of "What if it fails?" "What if they do? What if they don't?" or "What if I can't?" On the contrary, I love to live life on a grander scale (which frustrates a lot of people) "What if my cord closes before their very eyes?" "What if I walk again?" "What if I run again?" "What if I can finally write that book after all?" "What if this client says yes?" With God, I lead a WHAT-IF LIFE. I have been able to pull off many great feats in life and in business holding faith over facts and being committed to a "what if" lifestyle. Have you ever heard the phrase "The devil is in the details?" The devil is also in the facts. When the facts want to play over and over, just say to the author of those limiting facts, "What if, what if, what if!"

What are the facts holding you down? Facts turn into lies. Their voice says things like never, could have, should have, not you, not now, you missed your boat, no one recovers, and you will never succeed. Maybe the fact is that a woman has never held a particular position. Do the facts suggest that you will never recover from a broken heart or financial ruin or a shattered family? *The facts are full of fear, but faith says to fear, "Sit down and shut up!"*

Even the faith-filled experience sidebars in life. In the courtroom, when one lawyer calls for a sidebar it is a disruption in the protocol of the trial, a disruption in the rhythm of the process to reach a verdict. It usually means there is an "issue." Nevertheless, sidebars happen.

SIDEBARS

Finally, after several days of distractions, which I refer to as "sidebars," to my ultimate goal of walking again, we began therapy. The nurses came in and sat me up in bed. Struggling to find three quarters of my body in space was shocking. A slide board was used to help me transition from the bed to the wheelchair. The slide board was just that—a board that was very slick. They slid the board under my hips, slid me across into the wheelchair seat, and then slid the board out from under me. It made for safe transition.

As they slid me off the bed, the feeling of having no control of three quarters of my body in space sent tears streaming down my face. It was frightening! I was totally dependent on these women to keep me from becoming a lump of flesh on the floor. As I wheeled myself out of the room for the first time, there were more tears. "Is this seriously my life? Is this seriously happening to me right now? I am in a wheelchair and cannot get half my body to function?" For forty years, my life consisted of action, movement, athleticism, running, jumping, dancing, high kicking, and teaching others to do the same. Now I was in this place, desperately dependent on others to show me how to be me again. But I refused to grieve. After all, wisdom had said this was a birth!

NIGHTTIME RITUAL

It was a fairly cold winter. There was sleet and even some snow during the time I was in the rehab hospital. Spending New Year's Eve in a downtown hospital was a little unnerving. For weeks, I had listened to Life Flight land and takeoff again. One particular night, I remember wondering how much that familiar sound would increase as people rang in the new year. I never got used to it. Life Flight missions meant one thing and one thing only: critical care. The landing pad was just past my room, and the sound of the helicopter blades coming closer and closer from far off in the distant, getting louder and louder until they hit the pad at Brackenridge next door was common. On this night, New Year's Eve, they came more frequently. The weekends also saw an increase in activity, but no matter the day, they came at all hours, morning, noon, and night. Tragedy is no respecter of hour or day.

It must have been about 2am when I awoke from the pain. The tractor trailer had fallen lengthwise across my lower body. My legs were crushed underneath, and I could not free myself. The pain was gut wrenching and one that couldn't be escaped. It woke me up, and I struggled to find the call button to the nurses' station. This would be their second trip down the hall to room 217.

"What's the matter honey? What can we do for you?" the nurse asked.

"My legs are hurting so bad that I dreamt an 18-wheeler had fallen on them. Can you please rotate me and take these pumps off my legs?" My sleeping arrangements were horrific. The bedtime ritual was one I dreaded, one that could not be escaped. Every layer on my body was there for a purpose.

The first layer was T.E.D hose. T.E.D. hose or stockings are an abbreviation for "thromboembolism-deterrent." They are stockings designed and worn to support the venous and lymphatic drainage of the leg. This means that when you are recovering in bed, they help stop blood clots from forming, and I was a candidate for blood clots. They have a grip like a cobra and extended up to mid-thigh.

The next layer was a series of circulation pumps that electronically squeezed my legs in and out, in and out, and worked in combination with the T.E.D. hose. Again, their aim was promoting blood flow throughout the night. They were strapped on like cowboy chaps and then cinched up. These too extended up to mid-thigh. Helping to foster the flow of blood back up to my brain, they were nighttime companions.

The new shift nurse came in and said, "My goodness I have never seen these pumps. These are really long" Lucky me! As uncomfortable and cumbersome as these apparatuses were, they still ran a close second to the final layer: the podus boots.

Podus boots are intended to prevent drop foot, a condition where one is unable to lift the front part of the foot, and the result is a foot that drags. My feet were strapped into what looked and felt like ski boots. Another accurate description would be moon boots—the kind astronauts wear. Seriously, these boots were atrocious to sleep in but critical in preventing the permanent damage that could happen to my feet if the muscles were not in the upright position. The boots were heavy and prone to fall over to one side or the other. Therefore, once I was suited up and booted up, the nurses engaged a heel lock that kept the boots in place, unable to fall left or right, twisting my leg.

The locks made me feel claustrophobic, which had been an issue for me for a long time. Some nights I refused to have the locks on just to give my brain a panic reprieve. Knowing I was locked into position was too much, and I would just take my chances on the boots not rolling. Inevitably, they would roll, and the writhing pain that ensued would prompt yet another urgent call to the nurses' station for help. (And, for the record, I got drop foot anyway!)

Moving my legs back into position felt like setting a broken bone back in place because of the sensitivity that developed from the nerve damage. But this particular night, the boots had not fallen over and twisted my leg. The nurse who rushed in to hear about my dream checked my legs, and surprisingly, they were perfectly in place. How could that be? I was hurting so badly!

"Let's roll you over, ladybug," a nickname one of the night nurses had given to me. "It is time for you to rotate sides any-way."

Even though I was down to a whopping 110 pounds, it took two of them to roll me. It was not my weight that required both of them, it was the careful precision with which a roll must be done. Moving a paraplegic body that goes into a full body spasm resembling a charley horse when moved takes precision. Spas-ticity is a common side effect of spinal cord injury. It's a feeling similar to the abrupt grip of a charley horse in your calf, but mine were felt from breast down to toes. Sidebars.

The doctor had given strict instructions, which were posted at the head of my bed, to "rotate every three hours" to avoid bed sores, and one had already begun. Shifting the pressure of my body against the bed was a requirement. As gentle and skilled as the nurses were, the pain jolted me every time they moved me. The only assistance I could give was to turn my head, grasp the bars that lined my bed, and pull on "three." One, two, three, and there I would be, suited up and ready for another few hours of sleep—if the pain held off. My faithful assistants would never leave the room until I was respectfully nestled under the covers. The multiple attendants who served me all knew it was not "lights out" until my brown blanket was draped across me. It was December, and those rooms got so cold at night. Sidebars.

To this day, I sleep with my covers pulled just over my nose, just as I did in those cold rooms. Maybe it's a result of the deep sense of security it gave at such a time. My blanket was nestled over my body and always near my face. Fur on one side, satin on the other, that blanket was the only reminder of the warmth of home during those dark nights. It became the soothing touch I desperately needed in order to close my eyes and rest. My friend Suzan had no idea the comfort that blanket would provide when she brought it to the ICU in a brightly wrapped package weeks prior. The nurses loved covering me with it, and some nights, I would roll it up in a ball, lay my head on it, and just grip if firmly in my hands.

WEEK 5 MELTDOWN

By the five-week mark, there had been plenty of time for sidebars to have an effect on my emotions. My right leg was bent behind me, and I could not get enough leverage on the handicap bar to pull myself up.

"Help! Somebody, help!" In an instant, three nurses were at my side. The five-week meltdown was inescapable, and it came on this particular day. The day was tiring, I had a blood pressure crash, my bowels were still not working, and Lauren had called me with a stomachache, crying for me to come home. Hanging up from that call, I was rattled. I headed to the bathroom and fell transferring from my wheelchair to the toilet. Thank God the nurses' station was just outside my door. Although I partially caught myself on the railing of the toilet wall, I had no strength or leverage to push myself up. I knew that if I let go, the full weight of my body would fall onto the leg that was positioned behind me, crooked. Thank God, Adrian, the male nurse, young and fit, was on shift. He ran in and picked me up. That was it. Sitting in my wheelchair in the bathroom, I began to bawl. This was going to be the day I subconsciously gave myself permission to lose it. It was all too much, and something had to give. I picked up the phone, called Greg, and dumped all of my emotions onto him.

The time away from home and family was wearing on me. Adding to this pain was seeing how it was all wearing on my barely four-year-old daughter. At night, while on the phone with her, she was whining and crying more and more. She wanted to be held by Greg while she talked to me on the phone. She would ask things like "Mommy, when you come home will you swing me real high?" It was tearing my heart out, but I did not want to be discharged from the hospital until everything possible had been done there to help me.

Once I had been in the rehab hospital for those first five weeks, it seemed that everyone was moving on with their lives. All this activity was swirling around me, yet my life was on hold indefinitely. It sickened me. It made me feel panicked and alone.

I have battled this sinking feeling on and off again since I arrived home from the hospital. I have had to sit with the feeling of being left behind as all of my friends were soaring to new heights in their careers. I have had to let go of the limiting belief that I missed my boat so my fullest potential can still be unleashed within the time I have left on this Earth. Believing that your best days are gone because of loss and immense disappointment is a real battle. But that limiting belief only gets to play out in your life *if you allow it*. The renewal of that recurring toxic thought cycle says, "Indeed others have been experiencing success as I have been managing the fallout of unexpected outcomes, but better days are ahead. In fact, my best days are ahead because I know how to do hard things and how to thrive my way through them." God can restore what has been stolen in an instant.

Battling the sidebars of life often is more miserable than the effort required to reach the ultimate goal. It seems that having to fight for our future should be enough, but we also find ourselves battling for our today. As I battled for my mobility, I was sidebarred with distractions and interruptions to reaching my ultimate goal. And it is at this point where I must be completely transparent. If not for prayer and the knowing of God's powerful reality, the sidebars could have taken me out. Especially in my earlier years when my faith was not on track, this knowing kept me from being found in a ditch somewhere. Jesus saves!

What are the sidebars of life that are keeping you from reaching your God-given destiny? Is it the company you keep? Is it a job you should have left long ago because you are capable of so much more? Maybe it is shame and guilt from the past that has stolen your confidence? Is it unforgiveness that has spread through every fiber of your being? Chronic pain has been a sidebar of mine. Bed sores were also a sidebar while I was in the hospital. You get bed sores from lying in the same place too long; maybe you have been lying in the same place for far too long?

Sidebars are a hassle, and they are inconvenient, but they contribute to the sum of the parts—the whole person, the whole goal, the whole story, the whole journey. "But I will not grieve! Wisdom said this is a birth!"

Sidebars are a part of living. The very best advice I can give you is to surround yourself with professionals as you pass through deep waters. Pour your soul out before the maker of heaven and earth. He alone has all comfort and all grace. Be proactive in building a fortress around you. Also, make sure you are surrounded by cheerleaders as you maneuver the sidebars of life.

CHEERLEADERS

When I was younger, one of my favorite things in all the world to do was to cheerlead. It was exuberant, and it gave me the opportunity to get out an extraordinary amount of energy, excitement, and emotion that I carried with me from the birth canal. Not to mention, I grew up in the heart of Texas football country which, in and of itself, was gospel.

Entering into the hospital, I had a squad of cheerleaders who had my back. They were the ones who raised the deductible to cover my initial hospital stay with lightning speed, the ones who gave me that fur and satin blanket that was the only semblance of home through two months of cold nights in the stale rehab hospital. There were others who showed up with new pajamas and protein smoothies.

Can I tell you a bit about my head cheerleader? You've already heard a lot about her. She was my daughter, Lauren, and she turned four years old days before my surgery. Lauren was laser focused on my recovery. Cheerleaders always have words of encouragement, and Lauren was no exception. On Christmas Day as our visit ended, I heard, "Mommy, I am going to cry happy tears when you come home. Mommy, I love you with all my heart!" it was like jet fuel to my determination.

There was a period of about a month after I arrived home when I had to get injections in my stomach to ward off blood clots. Each night, my husband and Lauren would gleefully climb on the bed for our nightly injection routine. They were always a little more excited about it than I felt necessary, but nevertheless, Greg would stab the long needle in my belly and Lauren the Cheerleader would say, "It's okay, Mommy. It's okay." Encouraging words. We sometimes think that "just" an encouraging word can't mean that terribly much to someone suffering trauma, but clearly, I remember every encouraging word as if it were said only yesterday. Those encouraging words lifted me up and were important enough to write about in a book, years later.

The most encouraging words I probably ever heard Lauren say were said one Easter morning. She and I were in my bedroom preparing for an exciting day with family and her cousins. Lauren was sitting on my bed in her blue and white polka dotted dress, wearing a hat with white ribbons that streamed down the back, her little blonde ringlets bouncing out from under the sides of the hat. She also wore white leotards and fancy shoes.

As I finished my hair in the bathroom, we talked back and forth. I walked out of the bathroom and over to my dresser, and I heard Lauren begin to shriek. The tone in her little four-year-old voice was all at once full of elation, fear, and emotion. She was yelling, "Mommy, you are walking! You are walking, Mommy—where is your cane? You walked!" I indeed had walked out of the bathroom, mindlessly abandoning my cane and walking over to the dresser. It was a moment of thrill neither of us will ever forget. She and I claimed that I rose from the grave on Easter morning!

During my first few weeks home, Lauren had watched me take a couple of terrifying falls. She had seen the fear in my face and had an awareness of my inability to stabilize my wavering leg muscles. Her having to once again run for her dad to tell him I had fallen was not okay with me on any level. That Easter morning was therefore a special moment that built confidence in my heart, and in her little heart also.

I also had a different kind of cheerleader supporting me: my mom. A cheerleader from the past. I lost my mom to a rare form of Leukemia when Lauren was only four months old. It was a devastating, out-of-the-blue sort of loss. She was checked into the hospital on February 13, and she passed away in the hospital on March 12.

My mother was my female hero and the glue that held our family together. My mother was the strongest woman I knew (other than her mother), and they both radiated unconditional love, compassion, and forgiveness. She was born to be a mother, and we had an exceptional bond. Through ministry, I have come to know that many people do not have the luxury of having a "mother of all mothers," but I did. How I needed her during this time! I longed to talk to her in the hospital. Lauren needed her support and care while I was gone. There were many precious people caring for Lauren in addition to her dad, but no one suffices like your mom. Mother's cheerleading from the past shored me up on every side. My mother taught me and demonstrated victory in the face of daily adversity. Her strength and courage not to give in transferred to me long before I was in the hospital. Without words, she taught me to fight for what was important in life. Her virtues were selflessness and unconditional love. My mom was the one person on the planet who wholeheartedly understood me. Through all of my crazy adventures and gut-wrenching mistakes, she supported me and could always see through to the core of who I was made to be.

Lauren and I visited her once when Lauren was about three months old. As we were chatting in the kitchen, she said, "Amy you are a really good mom." I absorbed those words with every cell in my body. I have cried happy tears over those words more than once, words that never could have held such weight coming from anyone else. I put off having children because the enemy of my soul convinced me I wouldn't be a good mom. Yet, it has become the delight of my soul. Her many prior years cheerleading infiltrated the walls of the hospital day-in and day-out, accomplishing exactly what I assume she had purposed it to do: support and encourage me throughout the remainder of my life.

One of my dearest friends called and announced she would be at my house the following Saturday for retail therapy. It had been way too long since I'd indulged in *this* kind of therapy! She said she had a plan, and wheeled me up to Dillard's, heading straight for the cosmetics section. Lisa was sure that if she pushed me from brand counter to brand counter, we would be showered with cosmetic samples. If I remember correctly, her repeated pick-up line was, "This girl has been paralyzed and in the hospital for two months. We need to get her feeling beautiful again!" We left with a few purchases and a lot of samples!

The next stop was the furniture store. We left having gotten a great deal on a new Tempur-pedic mattress for my ailing back. I think we also left with a new sofa and chair. We called my husband to come and pay the bill, and he showed up less than amused by our wheelchair outing. It was truly the best day!

It would be an injustice not to give credit to the cheerleader we called to pay for our purchases that day. Greg, my husband at the time, was a strong and courageous servant to me. He lifted me from the shower chair to the wheelchair, he cleaned the porta potty, and he gave me shots in my stomach every night for a month when we arrived home. We laughed together as I sported my Depends diapers. We could just look at each other and, without words, know that both of us were thinking, "What on earth has happened to us?" Greg carried a huge load well before the surgery even occurred. During the months leading up to surgery, he was handling the housework, dinners, running a new construction company, and tending to Lauren because my pain would knock me out by late afternoon each day. He pushed me in my wheelchair through the streets of Baltimore as we visited Johns Hopkins. He lugged my bags (and his) through the airports. I could go on and on.

Greg and I shared a love for healthy living and activity. When that level of activity we were accustomed to ended in my life, I know he suffered that death too. He never made me feel guilty for the situation that he was suffering from; he never mentioned all the alteration that had gone on in his life for over a year leading up to that point. Little did we know, we were in for a heck of a long ride. He did the best he could with a devastating situation, and I am forever grateful, beyond grateful, for his love and willingness to serve both Lauren and me.

Who are your cheerleaders? Do you have that support system in place? If the answer is no, it is time to take a hard look at this integral part of your life. Don't be stubborn like I was in the beginning, unwilling to openly receive care and comfort from others.

On the flip side, there can be a tendency to blame others for our lack of a support system when we have possibly done one of a few of these things to put ourselves in that position. Perhaps we shut people out to protect our lack of confidence, or we feared that if they got too close, they would not be attracted to what they see. Sometimes, we know we are not what we have portrayed ourselves to be on social media, and we feel the need to withdraw. We also deflect people who are getting too close because of our pride or a false humility. The good news is that through my one-on-one work with women, I've seen the self-limiting beliefs that became cheerleader deterrents be brought to closure. Beliefs like "No one likes me or respects me or notices me or gives me credit" can be brought to a closure. If that feels familiar, I would love to support you past that roadblock, which almost always stems from vows made long ago out of a trauma.

I also realize that there are some of us who genuinely do not want to put others out by allowing them to serve or help us when we are in need. But, I learned something very powerful in my journey back to mobility. There are God-inspired assignments, and many times, those include serving someone else's needs. There are people who genuinely have the gift of serving, and refusing their help is denying them an opportunity to express their gift. We will all ultimately give an account of what we did with the gifts given to us.

These truths made a big impact on me. Understand that accepting help went against my own DNA, and there were more than likely several of the above examples in the mix that created my deflection. It honestly was almost a relief when I learned how to say yes to the people asking if they could cook for us, drive me to therapy, take Lauren out for a playdate, and on and on.

Maneuvering this thing called life is not a solo mission. Isolation is your enemy! That truth is why the temporary solution to slow the Covid-19 pandemic made so many people slip into depression, fear, anxiety, and even death. It has taken me a long time to learn this, and even with all my attention given to it, I still sometimes find myself drawing back into my "I've got *all* of this" mentality. My "I've got *all* of this" burden was birthed from a vow I made as a child, and it's one that is not life-giving. There is nothing wrong with having an "I've got this" mindset. But, "I've got *all* of this" is a heavy cross to bear, and you will never do it as well or as completely as you would if you were doing life with those God has sent to cheerlead on your behalf.

Another important thing I learned is what to do when you see someone in crisis or turmoil. With good intentions, we ask, "What can I do for you?" The answer is almost always, "Nothing. We are fine." Look around and see what is evidently needed and then either do it, offer to do it, or do it anonymously. For example, if the grass in someone's yard is a foot tall, mow it. If there are kids who need to be picked up from school, give them a schedule of when you can handle pick-up. If there are medical bills to be paid and it is Christmas time, collect a fund for the family. This is what I did for a family at my daughter's school when the dad had been out of work while battling cancer. Roll their trash cans in and out. You get the picture. If you really want to do something, simply look at their life and the needs will come flying towards you. Look for the obvious and get it done. Hands and feet of Jesus, people!

As loving friends, we want nothing but to come to the rescue of those we love who are in crisis, right? This is a long chapter, I know, but I want to deliver some sound advice having experienced multiple traumatic, unexpected outcomes. From being a cheerleader to others to being the recipient of cheerleading, my goal is to remind myself and you of some of the "best practices" for cheerleaders.

Many years back, I was a cheerleader for people I loved, but I approached my responses to them irresponsibility. In the end, we don't know what we don't know. But out of ignorance, in an effort to support friends I allowed my mouth, energy, and behavior to add more drama to their drama. (Remember, we respond to others' crisis out of our own refined or unrefined solutions to crisis. So, be cautious about who you confide in when seeking advice during a crisis.) After this approach was imposed upon *me* during one of my own crises (more than once), I began to realize the difference between helpful support and drama-creating support. Some cheerleading encounters leave me feeling empowered, supported, and connected, while others leave me with an anxious and unnerved feeling, even though, in each instance, the cheerleader on my behalf had good intentions.

Most people need support, love, and a "knowing" that they are not alone in crisis. What they do *not* need is more "stirring the pot" of whatever has happened. In other words, more suspicion talk, or drama talk, or fuel-to-the-fire talk, or what if talk does not serve them. The question we can ask ourselves is, "Is my friend better off after she leaves our encounter?"

They do not need a tactical overtake of the situation they are facing, either. Consider how they are experiencing you on the other side of you! We want to side with our friends, and we should. But this can be done from a stance of grounded, level-headed support. Walking away from a cheerleading encounter with the recipient knowing they are not alone and that you are willing to help figure out whatever they need is incredibly life-giving. Invading their space any further is usually a disservice.

Most importantly, *it is quite possible that others do not handle crisis exactly the way you do.* For instance, I am incredibly private about any crisis in the beginning. That has always been my truth. I just do not immediately air my dirty laundry. In that privacy, I am processing, praying, not jumping to conclusions, and attempting to stay level-headed. I allow a moment to see how something plays out before I start talking about it. My initial mindset is that contacting my friend base and going over the story repetitively will bring additional stress and burden. So, early on, I share information on a "need to know" basis. It keeps my thoughts intact.

My next step is to reach out to a professional and friends. Eventually, I'll speak to every detail on stage or write about them in a book! Other styles are to instantaneously run to every friend and start discussing the situation, and this style is helpful to some people. But, in any circumstance, commiserating over what already is happening is not life-giving.

Teenage girls do this in an effort to learn the best practices of serving a friend in crisis. I have watched my teenager and her friends work this through. In the beginning, they involve every ear that will listen, and the atmosphere quickly turns to frenzy. They do not use the kind of calm, stable voice that adult women need in crisis. They eventually solve the crisis with calm, but it takes a minute. Sit with this, and as my good friend Jan Goss Gibson would say, "Prepare to show up well, cheerleader!"

I have one final story that is so worth sharing. A very close friend showed up bright and early one morning at my front door (as a suggestion, maybe don't do this to a casual acquaintance). Lauren and I had just moved into our new home without her dad and my husband of eighteen years. Yes, the hits just kept coming. Despite the genuine cheerleading Greg did during my crisis, we had unfortunately battled differences on again and off again for years prior to my surgery. My eighteen-year marriage came to a shocking end, and before I could blink, Greg was married to another woman.

It was a dark time for me. My friends can attest to me saying on many occasions that this unexpected outcome rattled me more than paralysis did. I suppose I felt that way because of the loss I felt after intimately walking through eighteen years of intense life occurrences with one another. We experienced our once-in-a-lifetime spiritual awakening together, shared a deep friendship, shared a miracle child together (Lauren was born by emergency C-section after presenting with signs of distress in the womb), two miscarriages, the abrupt loss of a parent, the building of a company together, multiple emergency encounters with Greg's intestinal blockage and a broken neck from a bicycle accident, my tumor drama, and a lot of loving, extended family involvement. Eighteen years is a lot of life experience to intimately walk through with someone. It was a time of emotional paralysis for me, and the best I could do was get myself to my new nine-to-five job and Lauren to school each day. I did not have the energy or brain power to get my boxes unpacked.

My friend sensed this, and early on that Saturday morning she showed up with Starbucks and a stress relief candle and said, "I am here to put your house together. Get dressed; we are doing this now." Honestly, when she arrived *nothing* in me wanted to agree, but I did. I thank God she showed up that day, or the boxes would likely still be sitting there. We started ripping through boxes, and piece by piece we either placed each item in a room, on a wall, or in the garage to be donated to Goodwill. Cheerleaders know the team, and they know when the team is down.

Ask yourself who your cheerleading squad is. Get clear on who makes up this group for you. What types of personalities do you need surrounding you? One of the top things women say when polled is that they are craving relationships with other women. True relationships that are transparent and unconditional. If you are alone, ask someone to coffee. Take the initiative to build your dream cheer team. Don't wait for them to come to you.

Do you have a head cheerleader? Who gets you from point A to point B in the game of life? Please immediately go out and become a cheerleader to someone else. There are people right now in your life who need an encouraging word. Ask God to reveal this person to you—this action is more important than you will ever know. *Honestly, the simplicity or grandiosity of what you offer does not lessen or dramatically enhance the effect it has on the one in need.* People will never forget what you did for them, however great or small. The transitions of life, if they are to be accomplished successfully and with joy, must include cheerleaders.

Cheerleaders run out in front of the team, shaking their pom poms and screaming at the top of their lungs. They paint banners with words of victory and hang them from overpasses. **Cheerleaders stay until the game is over!**

POINT OF IMPACT

I learned something from my spinal cord injury that confirmed what I teach to individuals through Souled Out Ministries: At the point of impact, the sum of the parts breaks down. Between my brain and my feet, the control tower went down, and sidebars began to present themselves. My bowels shut down, the nerves to my bladder were obliterated, my hair began falling out in clumps in the shower drain, and my endocrine system went into chaos mode.

Damage spreads from the point of impact. An ependymoma tumor had invaded the control tower of my body, and all attached systems were affected. Moving on without addressing the overall damage would ensure certain loss of function and mobility. In short, refusing to look at the damage leaves unresolved pain—in one's body and in one's life. Anything unresolved must be resolved before the ultimate goal can be reached. Do you need freedom? Do you need healing? Are you sick and tired of being sick and tired but can't get a handle on it? I've been there, my friend—more than once. Are you hitting a ceiling on the way to your next-level life but can't imagine that your personal life could have anything to do with your work life or that your spiritual life or past could have anything to do with your professional success? If so, I designed The Freedom Success Method™ just for you, to help you get rid of the mental and emotional obstacles that keep you from achieving your ultimate best. The Freedom Success Method™ gives you the opportunity to super-charge your efforts, rewire your brain for success and happiness, and let go of the pain that is locking out peace and confidence!

Your next-level life and maximum mobility lives just on the other side of your biggest problem, obstacle, or pain stemming from the point of impact. A barricade has been constructed. There are structures in our lives that have been built and must come down. At the time these barricades are built, they seem to be good ideas to protect yourself. But at a later point, they no longer serve you. Ultimately, we arrive at a crossroads at which we need to address points of impact, and if we don't, we will never walk again in that area of our life. Addressing it can involve the slightest shift of a belief system or the complete overhaul of a mind out of control. The best formula I have ever followed is "find it, feel it, express it, heal it." This approach ensures that you do not try to stuff it away and move on in hopes that "it" will someday vanish. Your cup only has so much capacity, and it eventually overflows. I often attempted to skip the find, feel, express stage and go right for the heal stage. But skipping over the reality of the pain inflicted is a mirage. I was hitting a wall I could not get past. Acknowledging the pain inflicted to a trusted person, out loud, is not only healing in itself, it also allows the brain to accept and direct healing. God is fully aware of your pain. Take it to Him. Experiencing comfort from God is a powerful moment in time. Journaling can open the door to this two-way relationship.

In coaching individuals who are pursuing freedom from lockdown, I am known for emphasizing the need to "live radical for a season for a lifetime of fulfillment." I have tested this more than once!

Maturity says this TV is going off, the happy hour with toxic opinions ends, Facebook is on sabbatical. For a time, to get mobility, to shake the darkness, I pursue promise, possibility, and commitment to a radical season of renewal, to energy not force. If you are in lockdown mode, you have to stop "trying" to help yourself. "I tried" is not a results-focused answer when you are suffering with paraplegia. And, this same process applies even if you are only looking for a basic life change. A fire must be lit in your core that goes rogue from the past and blazes towards a pursuit of reset and renewal from the inside out. ALL success is an inside job. Set aside the external shell and get *really* honest with yourself. You will not die. Your innate wisdom tells you when to push, when to slow down, and when to crack open. God will lead you to whatever you are ready for. He is with you. He is a force higher, stronger, and wiser. He is a covering of love and grace deeper than the universe itself.

As I continue to press in and pursue my own next-level life, layers get revealed and peeled back from a particular long-time-ago point of impact. When this happened recently, I was initially quite hacked off. I thought, "Really? Am I still not there? Do I still have to acknowledge yet another level that is keeping me from fullness? What does this have to do with excelling professionally?" The answer: everything! When you gain access to a part of you that is not lined up with the next level you are seeking—whether spiritual, relational, health-wise, or professional, it has effect on you, the whole person. One unit is incapable of being compartmentalized *if it is operating optimally.* So, what is my point? It is worth the work.

Facing the pain of the present is never as debilitating as trying to change the past. We have to give up hope for a better past. Your power is in the present. During a time of emotional crisis having suffered domestic abuse, an intervention specialist gave me a book: *The Precious Present* by Spencer Johnson. He also authored *Who Moved My Cheese* and *The One Minute Manager*. They are all small but profound books. I was quite young when I first read *The Precious Present*, and I struggled to deeply grasp the simple message of the precious present. Today! All we EVER have is today. All goodness, peace, and ability to be fully you exists only in the precious present.

Faith must be present in the pursuit. Faith is defined as "complete trust or confidence in someone or something." In my story, it is also defined as "despite my circumstances, I choose, by an act of my will, to pursue the possibilities of, it is, I can, I am, and it is done." Then hunger (the fire) has stamina to discover misdirection and adjust, stop, and realign. You *will* get unstuck. You *will* uncover sticking points that attached themselves long ago and are responsible—partially, if not wholly—for your current state of lockdown.

I had to go back and retrain and heal every system attached to my point of physical paralysis. And you, my friend, are going to have to go back to the point of impact and face down every sidebar that has been commissioned to paralyze your joy-filled, life-filled, success-filled future! This is not a process that forces anyone to relive the past. It is a process of awareness and reconciliation. It is a process that goes back to the point of impact and entry to serve notice to the enemy of your soul that his time is up. Prudence goes back to impact and seals off the entry that continues to spew destruction into every human system, body, spirit, soul (mind, will, and emotions).

At my point of impact, my bladder, bowels, and endocrine system were knocked off course. And, of course, my sensory and motor function were as well. We could not skip over those points of invasion and hope they healed themselves or ignored them all together and wonder why in the world I couldn't reach my next level. The point of impact must be purposefully tended to.

Just as the spinal cord is the connection hub for every system in the body, it is all connected. There is a way to do this that maintains the integrity of your mental health, but still allows you to face off and battle the enemy within. In fact, it *heals* the integrity of our mental health. The way is to become an *observer* or *eyewitness* of the entry point and assess the root damage or misdirection of valuable systems. This allows us to plant our feet in such a way that we receive revelation.

In life, there are occurrences that we might not label as trauma when they in fact are. Out of the mouth of my dear friend and therapist Tracey Brock came the truth: "There are many occurrences in life our body and brain take on as trauma, whether we label it trauma or not."

In an effort to limit the length of this book, let me simply reassure you that a simple, safe system involves detecting when your life took a giant leap (or even a small step) into an existence that made you feel less yourself. It involves detecting when a particular emotion became an obsession, or when your perception of the world became counter to the way you originally thought. Highly skilled professionals in this area report it often occurs between the ages of three to six. These moments have the potential to be identified as your "points of impact." Some are ridiculously obvious, like sexual abuse, and some are way less obvious, as though they happened in passing but then stayed and swayed you off course.

Identification, as an *observer*, allows us to clearly see and realign our mindset while applying a few simple brain techniques. The step of being an observer is the game-changing, healing step that allows vast amounts of clarity to come to you. The observer step allows your assessment to come from the present realm, allowing you to move past the past. The observer step rarely can be fully experienced without the guidance of an unrelated party and without a higher power guiding you. A higher power that sees you, knows you, and reveals the way out and up to your next-level life.

Everyone's exact point of impact varies. The point of impact can be a mental or emotional infraction. One thing, however, is the same no matter what: the point of impact causes a lot of pain! I have suffered chronic pain for as long as I can remember. It began as chronic neck pain in grade school that was brought on from an injury at birth. This was the pain I was attempting to receive treatment for when they "accidentally" found the tumor. That neck pain bled into the back pain that began in my late thirties from the tumor and remains with me today. Mixed with the physical pain were bouts of emotional pain.

If you can imagine, I have just recovered from double disk decompression surgery at the L5-S1 region of my back. This area of my back, unrelated to the tumor, had significant chronic nerve impediment from wear and tear over time. In a desperate attempt to eliminate even an ounce of pain I experience on a daily basis I requested the surgery! It hasn't proven itself fully, but a small percentage of relief has presented thus far.

According to statistics, pain affects more people in the U.S. than diabetes, heart disease, and cancer combined. Various reports list that over fifty million, but up to 100 million, U.S. adults have chronic pain conditions, an estimate that does not include acute pain conditions or children in pain.

How many people in the world have chronic pain? According to this estimate, more than 1.5 billion humans among the over seven billion on earth.

Also, between fifteen and 100 percent of patients with depression suffer from pain, strongly suggesting that pain brings on depression. Mental pain is a whole other issue, but it still qualifies as pain.

My back pain exacerbated the mental pain that I worked so diligently to heal. There are very few people in my life who are aware the length of time I have suffered from depression attached to my life of chronic, unexpected outcomes in conjunction with physical pain that began in grade school. My depression began as anxiety and then morphed. The first time a therapist presented the concern to me, it gripped me. The idea that my joyful, full of life, and adventurous self was depressed was incredibly confusing. But, the fact was true that I would find myself full of life one day—and then sinking into the sofa the next.

By the grace of God I have been able to implement tools that keep it from taking me under, including prayer, brain work, meditation, and activity intervention. I have also done ETT® (Emotional Transformation Therapy) at my lowest point, which was wildly successful. ETT® is a modality of psychotherapy that uses several techniques based on color and light frequency. The ETT center reports this to be a new form of counseling that rapidly alleviates emotional distress as well as physical pain. The term "transformation" refers to the unusual degree of change that occurs when ETT® is used.

Regardless of the pain you suffer, I am pouring out compassion to you right this very moment. Chronic pain does not allow you to be the person you know you are on the inside. It changes your personality, and those closest to you are often the recipients of pain's backlash. People often misjudge your mood as distant, intolerant, or sharp. And, then feelings of being misunderstood exacerbate the ever-present pain. So here is where I introduce to you the concept of "gracing yourself." Chronic pain sufferers, please extend grace to yourself. The pain and anger and frustration you feel from your pain only causes more pain, as you know. At any point of impact, we have to extend grace and love into that exact deficit point.

Fear, hopelessness, and disappointment are each birthmothers of depression. Each of them comfortably settles in at the point of impact. This is a huge reason that I talk so incessantly about the importance of both healing our brain as well as managing our renewed brain. It all starts there, even with chronic pain, whether physical or mental. And, it is the reason that I am creating a product suite for those of you desiring an essential guide to developing a powerhouse brain that works for you, not against you.

Please release the shame and anger you may be feeling for the life and the joy pain has taken from you. Pain has taken away almost half of the physical activity I would like to engage in! Most of my life hobbies were snatched away. And mental pain has stolen precious hours of my life when I could have been living in joy with the ones I love. It is terribly exhausting, so pain sufferers, we need to be masters of managing our schedule, adequately resting, and gracing ourselves. Those simple things have brought peace to my life and will make your life a whole lot better also!

Lastly, the pain you experience may be in your heart. There is a direct connection from your brain to your heart, both spiritually and physically. Attending to them both brings the greatest measure of healing. Unforgiveness that lingers from a point of impact is a toxic weed that grows and remains until it is purposely discarded. If you are waiting for a payback, you have not forgiven. An expected but unfulfilled payment is holding you in bondage. Let me promise you that human justice will not set you free, but grace and mercy will. Cancel the debt owed (Eph 4:30-32). All we have to do is hear from families who have experienced violent crimes, and learn that leaving the court room having heard a guilty verdict put an uptick in their heart for only about two minutes.

Forgiveness is central to being made whole, and the habit has to be built within (because practically every day we need to forgive someone or something, however great or small). Unforgiveness can ruin your life as you attempt to hold court over the one who harmed you. The point is that we firmly grasp unforgiveness as a way to be set free from injustice, and ironically it is what keeps us captive, not the perpetrator of the crime. Forgiveness is rarely a one-time occurrence; it sometimes has to be repeated daily until the fruit of forgiveness manifests. Further, it is an act of our will long before it becomes a feeling. Forgiving a perpetrator is for "our" freedom. I have seen the fruit of forgiveness unravel decades of dysfunction in the lives of individuals who had no idea unforgiveness was their nemesis. Oh, and friend, you are also going to have to forgive yourself. Forgiving myself was a monumental task, but I got it done with an ever-growing awareness of grace from above. Grant yourself permission to be forgiven. He forgave you long ago.

In truth, unforgiveness separates us from God and from others, and keeps us in bondage to pain. If you are finding the release of unforgiveness impossible, I have an amazing handout that will help you through. To gain access to it, just email me at amy@livewithamy.com.

I promise, there is always a solution to bring greater healing to your point of impact!

AN UNLIKELY DAY

On a lighter note, pull your head out of the toilet, sister, your breakthrough is just around the corner!

Christmas was in the air everywhere except Room 217. My therapists were planning a practice session of transferring me out of my wheelchair and into a car. Surprisingly, the doctor had given me a pass for Christmas Eve and Christmas Day. I would be released to spend a few hours both days with family—if I could make it. I could have easily passed on it had it not been for Lauren. Frankly, the hassle and stress of being outside of full care was daunting.

The therapists needed assurance that my husband and I could work as a team so as not to injure me during the car transfer. As soon as they met Greg, who is six foot two, weighs 210 pounds, and has about five percent body fat, most of their concerns melted in a minute. Greg could pick me up single handedly and place me in the car in one fell swoop, even though that wasn't really a hospital best practice. With success, we were ready for Christmas Day.

Of course, I was up early waiting for Lauren to come through the door, excited and ready for all that Christmas Day holds for a four-year-old. My entire family was waiting at my older sister's home for our arrival. As I waited there with my wheelchair and meds packed up for the day, I was so glad I had agreed to make the effort to be away from full-time care, to take a short reprieve from the hospital grind. Coming through the door of Ange's house, the sights, sounds, and smell of the way we do Christmas washed over me. Ange made it so homey and traditional and wonderful. She had way over done her decorations and food preparation...just the way we like it.

The kids had already been waiting for an hour or so to discover what Santa left under the tree. As soon as they saw the wheelchair roll in, they knew they could dig in. Greg and my sister had gathered Christmas gifts for Lauren, and after watching her break dance in celebration after opening her Hannah Montana guitar set, I knew it was a success.

Family pictures were next on the schedule. We began gathering in front of the tree as we had done dozens upon dozens of times before. They rolled me in front of the tree first, as if I were the centerpiece of the picture. Feeling the impact of reality, I made a comment about the albatross of the wheelchair. My older sister, trying to make the day as perfect as ever replied, "It's okay, no one will notice!" As I burst out laughing, I said, "No one will notice the wheelchair? We all laughed so hard we almost cried.

For the previous thirty days in the hospital, I had not eaten terribly much per meal for a couple of reasons. One, I thought their food was gross and processed and, two, any morsel I placed in my stomach made the nerves light on fire. The pain in my stomach made it feel stretched like a huge balloon on fire. I ate the less rich food items on the table and hoped for the best. The one thing we did not consider was that I had been getting enemas, suppositories, and boat loads of laxatives for a month in an attempt to get my bowels working properly, to no avail. About an hour after lunch, all of those efforts succeeded.

When it hit, I was sitting on the sofa surrounded by family, and there was not an ounce of time to do anything about it. The second I felt my bowels release, utter panic hit. I felt it running outside of my brief and into my sweatpants. For thirty days, I had been surrounded by nurses and technicians ready to change and diaper me in a flash. My older sister was about to become Nurse Ange. She and Greg grabbed a towel, placed it in the wheelchair, transferred me to the wheelchair, and got me to her master bath as quickly as possible.

The embarrassment and disgust consumed me. "This cannot be my life!" I thought. "How much more humility do I need to experience?" God bless my sister! She sat me on the portable toilet that we brought over for the day and got me out of the diaper. As she attempted to clean me up, she had me stand up from the toilet, pivot, and lean over it. As I got into position, my hand slipped and my head hit the inside edge of the soiled toilet! We were both laughing so hard we could not get the grossness cleaned up for several minutes! You know the saying: "Better to laugh than cry!" When we finally caught our breath, I said, "Well this is going down in history as the 'Sh*t Christmas' for more reasons than one!" She rolled me out of that bathroom, and we carried on like strong women do.

My evening meds came due, and that meant it was time to go back to the hospital. Leaving my family was so hard. For a few hours, a hint of reality had dimmed for me. Now, pushing past Lauren in her Christmas pajamas and tousled white curls, saying goodbye made me sick inside. As we passed the table where she was playing card games with her cousins, she said, "Mommy, I love you with all my life! Mommy, I'm going to cry happy tears when you come home." It was gut wrenching.

One minute your head can be in the toilet, and the next minute your miracle shows up.

The next morning, I awoke—still exhausted from two days of holiday involvement, transferring, traveling, and generally being out of the controlled environment I had been in for a month. I was spent. The morning nurse arrived and informed me that the length of time allotted to have the blood clot filter implanted had been reached. So, it was off to Brackenridge Hospital to remove the vena cava filter. With a heavy dose of anesthesia, it was successfully removed.

Back in my room, dehydrated, exhausted, and still somewhat anesthetized, my therapists arrived on cue at 2:45pm. Obviously, my description to the nurses about my past few days' experience was not convincing enough for them to let me stay in bed. My therapist Cynthia said, "Okay sis, we planned on trying the walker today."

"The walker?" I thought to myself. "You have got to be joking. Today is the day you pick to see if I can take steps?" I replied, "Okay, I will try!" Zechariah 4:6 says "'not by might nor by power but by my spirit' says the Lord."

In our weakness, He is made strong. On an afternoon like no other, when I was weak, fatigued, medicated, and unmotivated, they sat me up on the side of the bed. We made our traditional transfer from the bed to the wheelchair, and off they guided me down the hallway to the therapy gym. In tow were a walker and a plan to do what I was there to do in the first place: walk.

I would make the attempt at something I so desperately wanted to accomplish and was so deeply committed to. The decision, the declaration, the dedication…and now the moment! An attempt to move my feet in a somewhat forward motion.

Not on a day when I was refreshed, rested, and invigorated but unexpectedly on a day when I was mentally and physically depleted.

One of my life pitfalls has been that I want all the conditions right before I do something great. Remember that polarizing perfectionism? I invite you to sit with this truth that I have learned: You and I can accomplish life-altering action in the face of adversity. Again, remember, the greatest feats are often accomplished amidst the greatest adversity. Life doesn't have to be perfect before you can get your miracle moment. In fact, it probably won't be.

We entered the gym, and they cinched my waist with a gait belt, which is a belt that serves as a safety measure to avoid falls. I braced my hands on the walker to bring myself to a standing position. They were coaching my every move, and then it happened! It felt like all my weight was on the walker, and while it was more of a scooching motion, my feet nevertheless moved forward. My destination goal was the exercise mat, which was about ten feet away. When I got to the mat, I sat down on it and cried tears of joy. Cynthia wept. My other therapist, Ellen, also wept. The moment was one that the three of us had each silently wondered about whether or not it would ever occur. The days that followed were full of cheers from the nurses and technicians as they returned to their shifts from the Christmas holiday to find me standing in the hallways, braced by my walker. "You're standing? Woohoo!" Some came in between shifts to say, "I heard you took some steps this past week...is that true?"

My favorite nurse came in and saw me on the portable toilet with the wheelchair across the room. She stood there for a stunned minute making sense of where things were in the room before she said, "Ladybug, are you walking?" I said, "Yes ma'am, with this walker." She said, "*Surely* the Lord has visited this place!" The "para" had indeed taken some steps, the Lord had surely visited, and it was all the buzz on the second floor.

RED LIGHT GREEN LIGHT

For the previous thirty days, she had seen me flat on my back. I stayed in bed when she visited because she could not stand seeing me in the wheelchair. It scared her. She'd say, "Mommy, get out of that chair, I don't like you in that chair."

The nurses' station and I knew the moment she arrived. The pitter patter of her feet increasing in speed were undeniable as she approached room 217. The hug I got as she hopped up on the bed was literally medicine for my soul.

After giving me a hug, she'd get super busy checking out everything in my room. She was fascinated with ice machines and loved to check out the gym where I exercised. Mom's room was full of fascinating gadgets. Her visits were priceless. She brought art projects from school, we colored, we watched Dora the Explorer, and we played many rounds of "High Ho Cherry O." My arms were covered with colorful wrist bands that gave critical instructions to the staff about me as a patient. Lauren loved the bracelets, and upon her visits would ask me to restate their meaning. As they got removed one by one, they began to serve as the countdown towards when I could come home.

She had gifted me her Christmas gingerbread house made at pre-school, and during each visit, I watched her pull off a few pieces of candy. By the end of my hospital stay, that gingerbread house had about two peppermints left and maybe one gum drop!

While it was hard for her to visit me in the hospital, Greg brought her every few days. She was right up in the nurses' business, observing as they checked vitals, administered meds, and drew blood. But, when she was done she was done. "Sorry, Mommy, but I have to go now...let's go, Dad," she'd say.

Every single visit was like this, but this day was going to be different. This was the day I would show her that I could walk.

She arrived, and after our initial hellos I sat up on the edge of the bed. Her eyes got really wide, and she asked, "Mommy, what are you doing? Mommy, where are you going? Are you coming home?"

"No," I answered. "I'm going to show you that mom is working hard to get better so I can come home soon."

"Come on, Mommy, get up! Let's go!"

The nurse came in and fitted me with the gait belt and the blood pressure corset. Greg cleared a path, and I began what I called my Tim Conway walk. Tim played an old man on the Carol Burnett show. That walk of his was legendary, and so was mine. A little shocked, Lauren walked ahead of me, protective. As people would pass by in the hallway, she'd hold out her hand and say, "Red light, Mommy, red light."

Once the person passed, she gave the go ahead by saying, "Green light, Mommy, green light." Finally, she looked at me and said, "Stop, Mommy, let me give you a hug. Good job, Mommy, good job! You are doing so good, Mommy." That was a great day.

TRANSITION HAPPENS

I t was right about that time that my cheerleaders showed up with gluten-free, dairy-free everything from Whole Foods (food happiness) and a card. The card was black, and it read "If you are going through Hell, keep going!" That is a card to post somewhere you can see it often while in the midst of sidebars and transition, and that's exactly what I did. I posted that card straight in front of my bed.

Transition is a given in life; if you are not transitioning you are six feet under. It is said in life the only thing that is certain is death. I would alter that to say that the only things certain in life are *transition* and death. Transition happens.

The only thing I have found that stays the same forever is Jesus Christ. He's the same yesterday, today, and forever more. I also feel like while my love for my daughter won't ever stop, even that love changes. With each passing year, I love her more and more with a transitioning of the heart that brings new awareness, new joy, and new levels of gratitude. You see, not all transitions are bad, and you will have a clear understanding of that by the end of this chapter.

There have been a multitude of transitions in my journey out of paralysis. It would take three more manuscripts to share with you all of the transitions of my life, what instigated them, and the outcome of each. There are a few key transitions I went through as I walked out of my wheelchair that I think can serve any human on the planet, and I'd like to share them with you.

The first thing to know is that transition is only for a season. We get knee deep in a transition, and it feels like it will quite possibly never end. Transition ebbs and flows. We find ourselves longing for a particular transition, and we resist others with every cell in our body. Regardless of which type you find yourself in right now, know that you *will* see light at the end of your transition.

In my work with women, they often find themselves telling me that they cannot figure out what is going on in their lives. They ask why they feel the way they feel, and why the approaches they have always taken aren't working anymore. Why have they lost their focus, drive, or passion? Many times, they are in the midst of transition.

My business coach shared an idea with me in relation to transition, and I have shared it with many to help them make sense of what is happening in the midst of their own transition. When a woman goes into labor, the first phase of that process, when she goes from zero to seven centimeters dilated, is the longest and least painful. She may not even notice the contractions. The next phase, when she's just nearing seven centimeters, she probably begins experiencing the repercussions of previous contractions. Heading from seven to ten centimeters dilated, a woman feels not only the pain of those individual contractions, but they seem to start running together with little down time in between. Shaking, shivers, or sickness could set in. That last phase is actually called the transition phase!

Just at the cusp of birthing new life, an incredible amount of pain must be experienced and managed. In addition, you must be surrounded with people who are just as smart as you are as well as some who are smarter!

If I were your transition business coach, this is what I would tell you when the depth of transition feels endless: Get in a new position. I mean physically, in terms of your countenance. Start walking with your shoulders back and your head up. Become aware of your physiology. It matters! Make eye contact with people. And, enlist someone smarter and more experienced than you when it comes to your transition type. Wake up at a different time, take a walk at night, speak out loud the exact opposite of the way you are feeling. We get into toxic syndromes and surrender our will. No more! You now know better. What is your countenance saying to the world? Stop once a day and review over and over in your mind the end result out of transition in its perfect form.

Remember, your brain believes what you tell it. It does not know the difference between actual reality and perceived reality. Search for a new perspective or reach out to a coach to get you across the finish line. Tunnel vision is a very real thing! Let a fresh set of eyes evaluate your circumstances. Don't jump ship until you have engaged in these practices.

Keep in mind, just before new life, new breath, new love is placed in the arms of a new mom, that mom is ready and able to break a human neck in half with her bare hands. That is the moment she knows she is about to encounter new life. In other words, her miracle is seconds away. Do you feel like you are passing seven centimeters and heading to ten? Congratulations!

Have you been praying for a transition to occur or complete itself? Have you heard about God's timing? I call Him my almost-late but always-on-time God! That is what transition can feel like—God is late, or possibly even going to stand you up.

The character of God is such that He completes the transitions of our life in perfect timing. This is one thing in life we can see only in hindsight, and it's the way trust is built.

The waiting through transition can lead to disappointments and frustration. Beware! It is in these moments that we all want to revert back to what is familiar and more comfortable, regardless of the dead end it has previously produced. To be human is to desire instant gratification, but doing so is self-sabotage. You are headed to your next-level life. Stop falling backward to comfortable but toxic. We must draw a line in the sand. So, here is a tip: If you want to wait well during transition points, do not abandon your value system. This is where you stand strong against life "happening" to you instead of designing the life you dream of. Hear me, transitioners! Sometimes, progress looks like failure. Sometimes, pressing forward feels like you're going backwards. Sometimes, healing seems like taking a step backwards. And, sometimes, a breakdown is actually a breakthrough.

My experience was that I would work, work, work, and then hit a plateau that ended up taking me down a notch. The therapist would instruct me to rest and return. Upon my return, I did not pick up where the plateau or dip had placed me; I actually picked up at a level higher than I was just before the dip or plateau.

It is quite likely that you'll find yourself in a situation you have never been in before. Waking up in the ICU, I didn't know what in the world I was going to do. No one does. That is what paralysis does to us. But, I since have transitioned to the point that I am able to help others walk confidently into the new space and the new day they find themselves in. Here are some helpful elements that you can enlist right now.

- Start figuring out your transition by being resourceful. (I began enlisting people smarter than I was about paralysis.)

- In the beginning, go with what you *do* know, not what you don't. (I knew how to physically train my body.)

- Cast your mind like stone that you are not going to bail. You are all in. You might need slight shifts, but you are all in. (I dedicated myself no matter the cost without seeing the future.)

- Look more intently at the breakthrough than the facts. (Keep your eyes on what you want and not what you don't want.)

- Get ready for grave distraction as you find new pathways. (It takes a minute to find new connections.)

- Expect new pains you have never encountered before. (Sidebars happen, so enlist a support system to ease the pain.)

I needed hand holding by a multitude of people and have had a vast army of professionals to learn from and strategize with. Success found me through my team of professionals who served as accountability, wisdom, commitment to the success of my journey, and straight shooters. Many times, these professionals practiced in an area in which I had much expertise, and many times they practiced in an area in which I had no expertise. This presents a mobility moment, and we often encounter moments like this in our professional lives. Can you imagine what could have happened if I had refused physical therapy because my pride said, "I know and should know the physical exertion portion of my healing." No. I moved right into Wheelchair City with humility.

If I do some quick addition, I'd estimate that I enlisted, post hospital stay, twenty-five professionals (and possibly five or six more I am inadvertently forgetting) who helped journey me out of paralysis to my next-level life. That is "professional enlistment," not friends and family, who have also been there, deeply caring about the success of my journey.

Some have remained on my team from the beginning, while others were there for just a season. But all have been pillars in my life book. All have been written into the fabric of my life. All are precious pieces of my life puzzle masterpiece. It's my mess of a life, or it's my masterpiece. My choice.

During this process, I have hit multiple dead ends that caused me to want to stop the story right then and there, which leads me to one of my favorite stories.

"I am tired of this story," said no one ever. The story to which I'm referring appeared in an excerpt from Napoleon Hill's infamous and classic *Think and Grow Rich*. It's a "golden" illustration of this very subject and is titled *Three Feet from Gold*. In transition, one of the most common causes of failure is the "habit" of quitting when one is overtaken with birthing pains that appear to be defeat.

So goes the story of a man who struck one of the richest ore mines in Colorado. Their first dig produced dividends. The next dig covered the debts, and the next would put them in "big time status." Before that happened, the dig that showed the vein of gold ore disappeared! They drilled on, desperately trying to pick up the vein again, to no avail. Finally, they decided to quit. They sold the machinery to a junk collector for a few hundred dollars and headed back home.

This junk collector was no dummy. He brought in a mining engineer to take a look at the ore and do a little calculating. The engineer informed him the dig had failed because the owners were not familiar with "fault lines." His calculations showed that the vein would be found just three feet from where they had stopped drilling, and that is exactly where it was found! That junk collector made millions upon millions of dollars from that ore mine because he knew enough to seek expert counsel before giving up.

Before success comes in any person's life, they are sure to meet with temporary defeat, if not failure. When defeat sets in, the easiest and most logical thing to do is to quit. That is exactly what the majority does. More than five hundred of the most successful men in our country told the author of *Think and Grow Rich* that their greatest success came just one step beyond the point at which defeat had overtaken them. Do not grow weary in well doing, for soon you will reap a harvest!

There have been a multitude of transitions that got me out of my wheelchair and walking again. I'm sharing with you these three because they will get you out of your "wheelchair" and on to your next-level life in a big way.

Transition One: From Home to the Surgical Table

HOPE

The first transition I had to conquer was getting from home to the surgery table. In this transition, I needed hope! This might seem like a no-brainer, but for me, it was terrifying. My pain was so intense that I could barely get myself to the bathroom and back to the sofa. Yet, my mentality was such that I was thinking, "Hey, I can still get myself to the bathroom and back. Why do I need surgery?" We all do this! Regardless of the pitiful state we find ourselves in, we hold on to environments, pain, relationships, and fear because we can "still take two steps to the bathroom and back." *I find it ironic that we are reluctant to submit ourselves to hope just because we cannot see the future*!

This tumor, this unexpected outcome, was calling for me to submit myself. To commit myself to the surgical table in order that I could find hope for a mobile future. At this point, I was doomed if I didn't and a little less doomed if I did. I had to leave the comfort of my home for the surgical table. My health was a situation that could not be remedied any way other than surgery. What was foreign to my body had to be removed.

Today, you have foreign structures taking up real estate in your mind, will, emotions, and spirit. These structures must be brought down in order that you find hope in these crippled areas of your life. Unexpected outcomes throw us into panic or shock that deteriorates to hopelessness. Is this your condition? You are going to make it through this, but you must, at all cost, choose hope.

I shared with you in the opening chapter the prayer I said while on my knees when wisdom met me the day prior to surgery. There on my knees, reassuring me, God's testimony was at hand. Within this transition, I held onto the hope that something out of this story would glorify Him. And now, twelve years later, I glorify a God who never forsakes us. *He gave me grace for the season—not deliverance but grace.* And, in so many instances along the path, He reassured me that He was still there. I knew that a testimony for Christ always has a good ending. God was there imparting to me that His testimony would be intertwined in this outcome. The fact that He had my back had to be reassurance enough.

Scripture names hope as one of the three greatest forces of human existence. Three things will last forever: faith, hope, and love (1 Corinthians 13:13.) God named these three as immortal powers. They are not just virtues inscribed on a plaque. They are mighty forces meant to carry your life forward, upward.

Faith and hope coupled together create resilience!
Faith + hope = bounce-back-ability.

Let me please speak into your life that hope can be found in any and every area that will lead you out of paralysis. His name is Jesus. He is the Hope of the world. The morning of my thirtieth birthday, standing on the street in the middle of my neighborhood, I submitted myself to hope. There, I submitted my broken and in-bondage life to the surgeon. Over a short period of time, God performed surgery on my heart, soul, and spirit, and He healed and cleansed the guilt, shame, perversion, lies, fear of man, lack of confidence, and abusive and addictive behaviors. Hope has also healed the deep sorrow and pain that's come from deceit and multiple betrayals in my life.

Hope on the surgery table. Hope on my knees. Both were places of submission. It is in the submission that we take hold of the hope promised to us.

Especially in business today, as our world has been altered by the Covid-19 virus outbreak. Millions of people are searching for hope. Quite possibly, within whatever profession you've committed to, you are looking for some renewed hope. There is hope on the surgery table where truth gets revealed; there is hope in submission. *When you choose to hope, you start to find it at every corner!*

How high can you hope today? Why or why not? We get to a certain point in life and want to accept feeling jaded. You must intervene in that and choose hope instead. What do you have hope in? Maybe it is the surgical table you need. Maybe it is a visit from wisdom. He is always talking. Are you listening? Really listening—from a state of submission? I met many people in the hospital who didn't have hope. When you lose hope, you lose everything. The thing is, there is always hope. *Hope is a renewable option available to you every single day.* Lack of hope is not a heart condition, it is a head condition.

You are birthing something along the way that will eventually produce fruit in your life. Some of our greatest awakenings, reinventions of self, and greater levels of development are birthed out of trauma. Purpose yourself to have eyes that see the birth and not what's been stolen. That is what hope looks like.

If you have lost hope here are a few practical things you can apply to watch hope come alive.

- Believe in a higher power than yourself to cast all your cares on so you can get them off of you and onto the shoulders of an omnipotent God.
- Set tiny goals that are very achievable. There is science that shows that having goals rekindles hope. We need to have a sense of where we are going and a plan of some sort (even if only in our minds) that gives us a sense of direction. It rekindles possibility.
- Have a conversation about the subject you have lost hope on or within. Two heads are better than one! Trust this.
- Find something you do have hope in and focus in that direction. It can be anything, big or small; the

process works the same way. It will clear the fog and allow you to revisit the hopeless situation with greater clarity and less despair.

Hope is a choice regardless of how you "feel." Chances are, if you are feeling hopeless, you are living in either the past or the future. Hope is found in the present realm, the here and now. The present is the true reality, and it's where you have power. When I am living in the past or the future, I start to experience anxiety, fear, restlessness, and even depression. There is no hope in the past.

Live in the present, look to the future, close the door to the past. This makes for successful transition.

Transition Two: From the Hospital to Outpatient Care

HUMILITY

Unexpected outcomes dump us in precarious places of almost always uncharted territory and unprecedented challenges. The transition from the hospital to outpatient therapy did just that in my life. Obviously, I was committed to staying in the hospital until I had gotten every single ounce of help and healing meant for me there. But, the obvious goal all along was to heal and transition to outpatient therapy, three days a week.

In the transition from the hospital to outpatient therapy, it is very important to know that I was checked in on the brain and stroke floor because the spine and trauma floor was full. The second floor was where God would do a mighty work in me, given that it was full of severely disabled, obese, mentally and physically incapacitated individuals who were, for the most part, elderly.

Upon her initial exam, the rehab doctor postponed my therapy. Her suspicion was too strong that I was at high risk for blood clots due to the lack of lower body function. That afternoon, I was whisked away for a procedure whereby something called a vena cava filter was inserted through my groin and up towards my chest. This filter's job was to catch any blood clots that might form and head for my heart and lungs.

As they were pushing me on a gurney to the hospital for the procedure, we passed by a room enclosed by glass. I looked past the glass wall into the room, which was full of my new cell mates. They were all partaking in an exercise class for the upper body. These dozens of hunched over, barely breathing individuals found themselves struggling to do even the motions of lifting their arms up, down, out to the side, and down again. This ex-athlete, runner, cheerleader, and aerobics instructor thought to herself, "Good Lord! Surely they are not going to check me into that class! What can they do for me in that class?" Can we all take a short moment and be astounded by how much pride we can possess, even when we're laid out on a gurney? A perspective redirect was coming my way.

Pride often blinds you from the real condition of yourself because pride must always see above reality! As the story goes, two weeks later, when I was strong enough to get into the upper body class, I found those cell mates kicking my butt, waiting on me to finish the exercise sets! I had lost forty years of physical training in an instant. Over the many weeks to come, I would be shown great grace by these precious geriatric floormates. They got to know me and my story, and I got to know theirs. A level of judgement I didn't even know I had was stripped away from me. Segregation left my heart, and a level of ignorance was peeled back and discarded.

There on the brain and stroke floor of HealthSouth Hospital, I found humility.

To be clear, there were other forms of humility, like being dependent for the basic needs of life and even to be rolled side to side in bed in an effort to avoid bed sores. I was diapered multiple times a day by male and female nurses. (They called them briefs, I called them diapers.) The process involved rolling me from side to side in order to get the soiled brief off, bed sores checked, and a new brief applied.

The enemas and suppositories never got easier. My bowels refused to start back up properly. Even with four laxatives and six stool softeners a day, I was not having proper bowel movements, and when I did the cramps would cause me to audibly moan and wince. The sensations were so distorted that I could not even tell if my brief needed to be changed or not. The most miserable night of cramping etched in my mind was a very low point during one of many nights I struggled through. A nurse I knew well came in to give me an enema and get me some relief. I was desperate for the medicine, but I also knew that once it took hold, my release would be in a brief that would have to be cleaned up by the nurses. She called for assistance from a male technician.

She first had to check for impaction. It was the middle of the night, and the room was fairly dark. I vividly recall being rolled over as I grabbed the leg of the attending technician with one hand and the metal bar of my bed with the other. As tears rolled down my cheeks, he patted my shoulder and I cried out to God. What a personal God we serve. After all, He made our bodies.

The anesthesia and heavy doses of antibiotics gave me a raging yeast infection. Initially, I had no feeling from my breasts down, so it was discovered by the therapist when she was bathing me. And, you got it, the nurses had to treat that also! The nurse for the week said, "I honestly haven't had to do this one single time in my nursing career." Both of us were mortified, but we did what we had to do! Girl Power.

When you are souled out to regaining your momentum, to scaling your wall, to climbing your mountain, things you would never do become welcomed tasks! It was a Saturday morning, and if someone did not give me a bath, I was going to scream. They had offered the night before, but I refused. I was too tired. But now, after four days with no bath, I was regretting that decision. My bath time was both welcomed and invasive. The night sweats left me literally drenched. The combined smell of my hair, my sweat-soaked pajamas, and the hospital were turning my stomach. After hitting the call button a couple of times, I finally heard the sweet sound of squeaky wheels coming down the hallway. A large blue rubber boat on a gurney, called "the blue canoe" arrived, and I knew fresher days were in sight. Getting my hair washed and body cleaned was so refreshing it clouded the part of my mind that would normally panic over two people (one male, one female) washing every orifice of my body.

The transfer from my bed to the "blue canoe" was always scary. After untucking the sheets from my bed, they would pull them up and wrap me in them, leaving just enough loose to grab and heave. My job was to cross my arms over my chest and lay very straight. On "three," in one fell swoop I would go from the bed to the bathtub. The next stop was the fourth floor, open-air, roll-in shower room. Passing the nurses' station in the blue canoe always got a cheer. I think it was a cheer of congratulations—maybe they smelled me too!

Extreme caution was used when pushing me on a gurney or in the blue canoe. The hard surface was a pain trap for the slightest bump we might encounter, and the bumps on the floor sent sharp pains through my spinal cord. The shower room was never warm enough, even with clothes on. Somehow, they got both the catheter and me on and off the wash table without incident. Capable of washing my hair, my underarms, and my stomach by myself, the nurses would, out of respect, let me do that part. They finished all other parts of my body, and as invasive as it was, I was eternally grateful that someone was willing to care for me, cleanse me, and return me back to bed with dignity.

Now that there are some irreversible images etched in your brain, let's discuss a more practical aspect of humility. A key part of my humility journey was having to welcome instruction in an area I had much expertise in, which was physical training. I had followed a passion for fitness my entire life, working in multiple gym facilities and teaching fitness classes. This was a subject I had studied obsessively, lived, and was looked at as an expert in. At one point in my twenties, I was even encouraged to enter fitness competitions and probably would have fared quite well. If not for my lack of confidence, I would have been a contender.

Here, I was dependent every day on others in the field of physical training to get me out of my wheelchair. The resemblance to business here is uncanny. Finding ourselves in a position to depend on, gain advice from, and learn new perspective from individuals in an industry we have played big in for most of our lives is humbling. The Covid-19 fallout has placed people in these sorts of uncharted waters. It is a space in which many are uncomfortable.

Your power stance is humility, which allows you to ask for help. The entire world is learning right now that the only way to successfully navigate this new existence is by asking for help and leaning into each other. Now more than ever, those who refuse will be left behind. It is hard to become the student in a class where you have been the teacher. Other than the mental fortitude I established through decision, declaration, and determination this was the ticket out of paralysis. It has remained so for the past twelve years, since walking out of my wheelchair, and it just may be your ticket to your next-level business life.

Humility—it allows us to become teachable, trainable, and promotable. Humility also allows us to be deliverable from bondage and destructive belief systems. What comes to mind when you hear the word humility? Do you think "soft and spongy" or "power and progression?" People are attracted to healthy humility without even knowing what is drawing them in. The Bible states that pride comes just before a fall! The lessons learned within the difficult and triumphant transitions in the hospital have remained with me to this day.

With hope on my side and humility allowing me to become a person of depth, I began my work in the outpatient facility.

Transition Three: Outpatient Therapy to Flying Solo at Home with a Trainer

HUNGER

I could see my running shoes sitting on the floor in the corner of the room. "I long to run," I thought. My baby girl and I had plans to run together. Weeks before surgery, Lauren received toddler roller blades for her birthday. We had plans to roller blade together.

This next transition was from outpatient therapy to flying solo at home with a trainer or therapist of my choice. It is within this transition that I learned the true meaning of hunger, or deep passion, and where it comes from. I was transported to the hospital on a forty-something mile roundtrip, three days a week, by my cheerleaders.

My precious friends put together a transport schedule and picked me up in their SUVs. Parked on our slanted driveway, they would hoist my wheelchair into the back. Every time, I would sit in the front seat, close my eyes and cringe, and ask, "Can you get it? Can you get it?" I felt so badly. That chair was so heavy and bulky—it had to have weighed fifty pounds-and they were loading uphill! I tried to remind myself that not allowing others to serve was stealing their blessing and not letting them use their gifts. It was not easy. We would head downtown to the hospital where I would spend two or three hours getting therapy in different areas. Parked out front in the wheelchair, I would wait for them, often watching as people zipped in and out of the double doors of the hospital entrance. I would watch their feet walk them in and walk them out, amazed by how everyone's legs worked but mine and how unaware we can be of that gift.

I participated in traditional gym therapy, then pool therapy, and then neurological function therapy. The pool therapy was fantastic. I transferred out of my wheelchair and into a seat on a lift, which would then lower into the water and drop me off. I loved the pool because it diminished my pain and gave me body control.

This transition from outpatient therapy to training solo was another transition full of struggle and emotion. During this short transition, I counted nearly 255 physical therapy sessions. Maybe I missed one or two of them. Maybe. I showed up energized. I showed up frustrated. I showed up inspired. I showed up hurting. I showed up refreshed. I showed up nauseated. But I showed up. And, it was in that showing up that a hunger, a fierce hunger, to reach my goals began to move me. I had a hunger to run, not just walk.

Results were starting to manifest from the hunger that committed me to keep showing up. Passion poured out of me during those sessions. My hunger was fierce, and fierce hunger allowed me to press through an all-consuming pain—pain that resembled a vice grip around my core that felt like it was squeezing me in half. Some days were great, and some days not so much. I had to adjust, adjust, adjust. I left each therapy session giving mental power to what I wanted the adjustment to be and how it would look and feel.

With every new discovery, we get hungry for more. It takes a minute to get your rhythm when starting a healthy living program, but with every pound lost or every better night of sleep, it gets easier and easier to fight for your health. It took me a minute to get into the rhythm of finishing this book. With each new chapter complete, I became hungrier to finish. That hunger demanded a process, and that process was to schedule habits week-in and week-out, including waking up at 5:30am, even during quarantine. It got easier and easier as my hunger grew to finish this book and get it into your hands.

My physical therapist often said most people do not surpass a certain point of healing because of the pain produced by getting back on your feet.

"The man who can drive himself further once the effort gets painful is the man who will win."
—Roger Bannister

Transition pains! There is an outrageous parallel to my journey of overcoming paralysis when experiencing any healing in life that we are willing to fight for. Fighting for our freedom in our body, spirit, or soul (mind, will, and emotions) can be a painful rewind with powerful, awe-inspiring results. This is what was unfolding in my life every time I showed up. The only way out of paralysis was to drive straight through it. It couldn't be side stepped or hopped over or stealthily ducked under.

Passion builds as we move. We find the hunger and fight we need to accomplish something great by moving, by taking steps, however dysfunctional they might look like in the beginning. *This perfectionist learned that progress is my perfection!* The alternative is the paralysis that comes from perfectionism, and there is nothing perfect about that. In taking these steps and showing up, *fierce hunger begins to demand a process*. That hunger begins to map out a plan and a vision. The plan that was birthed out of my hunger was to show up, speak up, and grow up.

SHOW UP, SPEAK UP, GROW UP

**If you show up, speak up, and grow up,
fear will shut up!**

As I reflect on other times in my life when I launched an all-out assault to overcome and heal the bondages in my life, I realize the processes I'm now teaching others were the processes that set me free and got me out of paralysis. That process included decision, declaration and dedication. It included the manner in which I showed up, it included a voice to connect to the way things were going to be, and at every new barrier to scale it included a new level of maturity.

Show Up

Eventually, the manner in which you show up is the manner in which you gain success. Over the course of twelve years, showing up to therapy every week (with very few exceptions), the therapist, doctors, and specialists took note of my countenance (how I showed up). Each new therapy destination landed me in the hands of supportive people who would repeatedly say, "You have an extraordinary outlook on your situation" or "Wow, you are really handling this well" or "Man, you've got a great attitude about this" or "Wow, you don't act like you hurt that bad-ly."

Where does that come from—being able to show up for over 1,100 physical therapy sessions with a good attitude, de-termination, commitment, and a smile more often than not? How did I consistently show up enthusiastically declaring, "Let's go! Let's do this people! I am ready for the hard stuff!" First, it came from the Holy Spirit living in me. Second, it came from a simple conversation with the hospital psychiatrist on what was perhaps Day Two of my journey.

RESOURCE YOURSELF

One of the first professionals I saw in the hospital (other than my assigned rehab doctor) was the hospital psychiatrist, whose job it was to evaluate patients' state of mind and emo-tions after a traumatic life event. They are there to discuss other things as well, but there was one primary topic he talked to me about. He said, "Amy, from this day forward, *you have to man-age your healthcare.*" He was saying, *Don't depend on the doc-tors or nurses or administration. YOU be in charge, forward thinking, and observant. If you do not, you will be the subject of others' preconceived processes and belief systems.*

He encouraged, "Continue to seek out the help that you need, and when you are not satisfied, look for another opinion. Do not depend on the doctors or anyone else to put your needs front and center or, for that matter, dictate what your needs are. That is up to you. If you do not get the answers or help you need, go to the next and the next and the next." I coined this process "resourcing oneself."

Always be resourceful in securing the resources you need. The combination of having God within me and this level of self-empowerment to manage my care has been life altering.

The advice that doctor gave me was worth more than gold. There have been many times over the past twelve years when I have had to be strong enough and mature enough and engaged enough to say, "This has served me well for a season, but it is time to move on." On to better-suited therapy, better-suited doctors, and expertise that was better-suited to my strengths and the deficits that remained at that point in my journey.

This system of moving forward is the reason I could show up every single week with a good attitude, a smile, and tenacity for the painful task of walking again. Because I knew, subconsciously, that I was in the position of management, and that where I was—for the moment anyway—was exactly where I needed to be. This knowing allowed me to show up "all in" for physical training, for mental training, for in-depth conversations with doctors about real time and next best practices for me. I was the one in charge, driven by the promptings of God *to resource myself* and choose the best place to be next on the way to where I was going.

There wasn't a bunch of self-doubt, worry, or deliberation. I innately knew that God was carrying me, and that I had done my part. Every single time the place I was could not serve me any longer, the next resource showed up like clockwork! It was already in me to be on watch for the next best thing and to sense when it was time to transition in order to gain maximum mobility. This was a stance of empowerment. Resource yourself! You will show up completely differently when this pattern for living is followed.

As I was recently training a group of women through Souled Out ministries, it occurred to me that this behavior perfectly transfers into our spiritual lives as well. Our spiritual life should employ exactly the same approach. We have to manage our own faith. It is not the responsibility of the pastor or our spouse or a family member or a prayer partner. It is ours and ours alone to manage. How much responsibility have you taken on for your spiritual development?

That development transfers into the other parts of you as a human, in body and soul (mind, will, and emotions). That, in turn, transfers automatically to your personal and professional lives. Had I not heeded the doctor's "resourcing yourself" advice, I honestly would quite possibly have been forever stuck, waiting on other people to tell me where to go and what to do next. Instead, I have made the tough decisions, have done the hard things, and have kept my forward momentum. No one knows you better than you know yourself! We would never allow someone else to be in charge of our professional success, of what job to take next, what retirement benefits are best for our family, how to interview, what skills to add for continued success, and promotions to apply for. Why oh why do we give up that power when it comes to our faith journey? There have been times in my life, however, when I was that person. Then, when I needed my faith and hadn't been managing it, my immediate thought was, "Why has it failed me?"

Resource yourself!

RESIST THE SOCIAL MEDIA STRANGLEHOLD

There is a new sheriff in town when it comes to coping mechanisms, and it is the use of social media. How are you showing up on social media? What does this look like when viewed by the other side of you? We are ravaged by the need to maintain a façade of what our life looks like through the eyes of fellow social media viewers. Are you in a social media stranglehold? Would you even know if you were?

Let me repeat here something that we have all heard: What you see on social media is the highlight reel, and many times, that is intentional. Let me confirm to you that no one—and I mean no one—has a highlight-reel life 24/7. It simply doesn't happen. If they are human, they also have a lowlight reel. On the flip side of my point that many people intentionally build a façade, that façade sometimes feels like taunting to some viewers. Certainly, I have fallen victim to this, looking at Facebook and putting the computer down depressed, disappointed, and bitter about the life I didn't have. I think we are way further along with understanding the pitfalls of social media for both adults and kids than we have ever been. We have been collecting data on it long enough to realize the negative implications can be as severe as death.

We must understand that most people see through the intentional 24/7 highlight reel, and that allows us to be released from the pressure that it creates in our lives. It's like creating one demon to cover up another demon, kind of like when spring rolls around and I look at my legs and say, "I need to go get some sun damage to cover up my sun damage." I'm sure you get the point.

The person with a "my life sucks" mindset must know that there is always a lowlight reel of someone's life that isn't being shown. This conversation I am having with you right now is so that we can illuminate maximum life in our lives and the lives of others our existence spills over to. It is about freedom! Social media "show up" likely isn't a point of paralysis for most, but it definitely is a stumbling block for many.

BE A WARRIOR

I'm hoping you took to heart the bit about how important it is to declare your habits in order to release yourself from paralysis. Habits obliterate the "trying" syndrome. Habits also build the kind of hunger that infuses passion. There are habits that warriors implement to ensure success in battle, to win the war. My particular war was on physical paralysis. Read closely, because this warrior mentality is perhaps not what you are accustomed to. It initiates a different mindset. Even us "A" types need to review this message, but it is included especially for those of you who feel weak or who have allowed society and the enemy of your soul to jerk you around for far too long.

There is a season for war faring. Look, your freedom is worth fighting for, and the fight I am suggesting is not meant to get you bloodier than you already are. The first thing to do is hit your knees! Pour out your weary soul. This gives you the strength to receive what I am about to say. This warfaring I speak of is as wise as a serpent and yet as gentle as a dove. This frame of mind and spirit required is not about mustering up force, but instead a framework of energy purposed towards freedom, discovery, and perspective redirection. You must be a warrior—in the sense that you are tenacious in your dedication to walk out of the "wheelchair" life has placed you in. You must be tenacious in your curiosity to seek the "true" reason you have not yet reached that next level in your life or business.

It goes without saying that there were many times I did not feel like a warrior while in the hospital as well as over the past twelve years. Certainly, I have felt hopeless and helpless at moments. There is a story in ancient script that tells of a man named Gideon. He was asked to go into a mighty battle, and in his angst an angel of the Lord appeared and called him a mighty warrior. At the time, Gideon was not feeling much like a warrior at all. But the angel of the Lord also told him a higher presence than himself was with him.

This is the case when it comes to your life as well! You are a fighter. Yes, you are. It is not a feeling but an ability. The ability to find your way out of paralysis not by force but by energy. Suit up. Here is how you begin.

First, you must "know" as a person of faith that, although we live in this world, we do not wage war as the world does. The weapons we fight with are not the weapons of the world. On the contrary, they have divine power to demolish arguments and every pretense that sets itself up against the knowledge of God, and we take captive every thought to make it obedient to Christ.

Second, you become an observer of every stronghold, every chronic thought that has held you captive, every structure blocking your GOD vision. What is God vision? It is vision that depicts a destiny for you that inspires every cell in your body!

Third, you take on the mind state of a warrior. I've thought a lot about how warriors show up. Warriors battle when they don't feel like it—wounded, weak, worn out, and in potentially horrible conditions. They are trained, strong, wise, and full of mental toughness. They war with a win column and a loss column, but they show up!

Many times throughout the Bible, these warriors were assured that God had already won the battle. Their job was simply to show up well. They were promised that He had gone before them and would be their rear guard.

Warriors go with weapons. Ephesians 6:10 says before any other weapon, we go with the Word of God that is the sword of the spirit. The second weapon has to be that of a well-disciplined and trained mind. If your mind is a toxic mess, pause and figure it out. Then and only then are you armed to take back your mobility.

Warriors go with confidence. Business leader John Maxwell speaks on confidence, and I once heard him say, "Focusing on your strengths and leaving your weaknesses to someone else builds confidence." Brilliant. We lose confidence because we cannot become a ten in our areas of weakness. We may always be a five in our areas of weakness. Leave your weakness to someone else, because you can be a ten in your areas of strength all day long! Make sense?

Warriors go with wise counsel. Resource yourself! Remember my team of at least twenty-five wise counselors? To this day, I battle with them by my side. Proverbs 15:22 says, "Plans fail for lack of counsel, but with many advisers they succeed." And, of course there is no greater counselor than our God...Psalm 16:7: I will praise the LORD, who counsels me; even at night my heart instructs me.

Warriors go with passion. You know it is passion when you must do it! You cannot *not* do it. Passion is the great energizer. You are not taking a vote or looking for approval. Passion equals energy. Lack of Passion equals lack of energy. Where you find an energy depleted person, you find no passion.

Warriors go with a plan. Hunger demands a process (a plan).

For what reason were warriors in history so incredibly committed to their cause? What were they fighting for?

They fought for freedom.

They fought for their future.
They fought to reclaim land they believed was theirs.
They fought to conquer evil.
They fought for heritage or generational freedom.

Warriors stay incredibly focused in battle. Their goal is to be able to shift to a desired frame of mind on a dime (which takes maturity and rehearsal). I had about two minutes to get lost in doubt or the land of "not" while walking out of the wheelchair life had literally placed me in. Then, because I had done the work of an observer and gained clarity about my self-limiting beliefs, I was capable of shifting back to warrior mode quickly. My mental strength also returned to me quickly because I was resourcing myself, reminding myself that I was where I was supposed to be for that season.

My teenage daughter is astounded by how I don't "freak out" about really big stuff in life anymore (most of the time). Honestly, I'm astounded as well. But, I am capable of keeping my brain intact, which keeps my emotions intact, which allows me clarity to take reasonable action that benefits my life and the lives directly in front of me. Through multiple life-altering, unexpected outcomes, I've trained myself over time to use the same truths and processes I have been sharing with you. I am now capable of showing up in warrior mode (again, most of the time). How do *you* show up when a teenager behaves like a teenager, or a boss makes a stupid move, or a team member does the unthinkable, or an extended family member acts like a stereotypical extended family member?

When we have done the work and aligned our soul (mind, will, and emotions) with positive action, we attain what I call *"freedom alignment."* You are now free to conduct life success-fully, because alignment has been achieved. Your mind, will, and emotions now mirror each other, and they are all pointing in the right direction. And, when they aren't, they can regain alignment quickly. I can truly say that, more times than not, I show up in a way that I am really proud of, and that, to me, feels like total freedom!

SPEAK UP

I have already poured my heart out about the power of declaration. Declaration became a powerful part of my success, but it wasn't about simply declaring my end goal. It was also about using my voice, my words, to intensify the results of my efforts through a mind-mouth-body connection. I knew there was a spiritual truth to this success, but at the time I did not know that there was a scientific basis for it as well. We are created for that connection, and it strengthens our results.

The challenges I was facing were enormous. Yet every time I spoke out my declaration, I got stronger. As I used my voice, I conquered the goal. It was like a drug to me, and it worked. "Step, step, step," I would say out loud as I was asking my brain to circumvent damage in the cord and make a body connection. "Lift, lift, lift."

Summer was upon us and Lauren needed a mom who could get in the pool with her, who could both climb in and climb out. "Mom's coming Lauren, Mom's coming!" I locked in my visual to get to my baby girl. My purpose was in front of me.

This is your process too! Newsflash: There is no way to achieve your next-level life without making consistent mind-mouth-body-action connection a habit. From both biochemistry and physiological standpoints, The Freedom Success Method™

teaches you how to find a lost voice and make this powerful connection.

Until now, you have possibly not recognized it, but there is a PHYSICAL RESPONSE to your words that is initiated through thought, which triggers a word, which triggers an emotion. It's science—every word carries an energy that can be sensed, regardless of whether you're thinking it, speaking it, hearing it, or reading it. There are high-energy words and low-energy words that you are using daily. In the chapter on "declaration," I gave as an example the time when I learned that the word can be as simple as "not." That one word was creating a lot of depression in my life. The small shift I came up with, based on Dr. Leaf's concept of brain health redirection, was to replace "not" with "it is good enough on the way to where I am going." The replacement statement that resonated with me was not blind to the fact that some things were not as I wished. What it did was take my focus off of "not" (low energy) and replace it with a higher-energy statement. This is an ongoing adjustment for me because I am always striving for more, and this bent in my innate nature can become a breeding ground for "not" unless I remain aware.

I was called onto the proverbial carpet about this very habit in the hospital. On more than one occasion, one of my many therapists would comment on what a bad habit I had of not celebrating small victories because it was "not." Not good enough, not at my expectation level, not what I had hoped for, not strong enough, and on and on. The "not" syndrome was rearing its head again through my mouth. And I was only speaking it because it had first been mulling around in my mind.

Let me debunk the lie that often presents itself to people of faith with regard to speaking up and using one's voice for destiny. At one time period in history, pastors got a bad reputation for "preaching" what was labeled a "name it and claim it" theology, which was basically a speak-it-and-you-will-have-it theology. For the purposes of this chapter, "name it and claim it" simply means you send energy through your mouth in the direction you want to go! You use your words to motivate your brain to take action. I call that smart.

The naysayers said Christians were being oblivious to the facts before them. Others can look at the facts all day long...I choose to look at how I can catapult myself under, over, or through the facts that do not line up with my vision, passion, or destiny, as God goes before me and covers my behind (it actually says "goes before and behind me," but in most cases, what I hear is "He covers my behind!"). We don't deny negative facts in our lives, but we will choose to focus on a higher reality: God's truth. Our affirmations are a tool that drives our vision towards success. What realm is your voice living in? There is a realm of higher power and vision, and there is a realm of the world's limiting viewpoints. One breeds success, while the other breeds discouragement and doubt.

With awareness, there is a new vibration available to our body and mind. With awareness, you can start showing up differently and taking different action that creates new results. All of this flips the script when it comes to how you show up. Otherwise, you are just creating more of the same.

The power of the spoken word is the confirmation and affirmation to support your resolve. Remember the resolvolution within our decision? Listen, the walls of Jericho fell by faith and a shout. By the use of their voices in due season. And, did you know that this wall was, in some places, twenty-five feet high and twenty feet thick? God has taken down walls that resembled this in my life, and He will do the same for you.

This is a pretty incredible story in the book of Joshua. Joshua, the commander of the army, commanded by God, was told that God had already gone before him to defeat his enemy. Joshua was also instructed to have non-stop talk and meditation on the right things, so they were practiced and ready for the moment when it would count.

Have you lost your voice? We lose our voice when we lose our value. We lose our voice when we are overcome by fear. We lose our voice when we don't believe we can. No one attaining their next-level life has a paralyzed voice, so let's remedy this!

Up until this point, I have not given a huge amount of weight to the "fear" of coming out of paralysis. It is beyond important that you know that I was *very* frightened at different times throughout the process. The key was, I moved forward anyway.

Much of the conversation I want to have with you about losing your voice came from my executive coach. She reminded me that one of the unique and defining qualities from our species is that we use words. Words are our Godlikeness, and they identify our humanness. Words allow us to step into that Godlike power. That is why such a void is created in our soul when we have words stuck at the base of our throat that we cannot get out. Of course, this can happen to all of us from time to time. But, there are some of us who have chronic paralysis in this area. The Freedom Success Method™ helps you drill down with life application techniques so that you can find your voice.

But, for now, let me share some key areas of focus that can get you moving! Let's be clear that fear is the underlying factor when losing your voice and your words, but any person can process their way out of fear and find their voice. Even you!

First and foremost, you must know without a doubt that YOU HAVE PERMISSION to speak. Your voice counts, no matter what. Your vantage point is needed. It is not stupid; it is not inferior. It is your power.

The speak-up step to your next-level life will always involve risk. But, as we covered earlier, we already know that life is one big risk. Yes, there are unintelligent humans who will possibly make you feel rejected, criticized, or embarrassed when you speak out. So what! Say it anyway. The idea is not to say anything and everything you think. It is simply to take a step towards a level of maturity that leads to greater success, to sit with our words and get better and better at using them to our advantage at a moment's notice.

Once your words are identified and you know what it is you really, really want to say, let go of the expectations you have of those who hear your voice. Their response is not your problem. It really isn't, as long as you use voice with responsibility. The great news is that you can always "revisit" what you said. It's far better for you to use your voice, speak up, and then have to revisit and restate a few things than it is to chronically live stuck in the corner. That's not happening on my watch. And, if you are in regret about what you *did* say in a particular conversation, "revisit" that conversation and speak your new words. Journal your words in order to be prepared, and speak them out loud to get comfortable even hearing your voice. You were not made to sit in the corner, regardless of what fear told you.

If you are going through life resenting everyone you encounter personally and professionally, it is time to scale the wall of fear and speak up. Resentment often reflects the disdain we feel from chronically not saying what we need to say. Chronically holding onto our words and internalizing them is very poor self-care. With the root of fear mixed in, we begin to see the results of this through a myriad of health struggles. Let me reiterate that is not a license to blast people with every word you can conjure up. But holding in your words is paralyzing half of you (at least) from fully living your life.

This is the forward mobility of *your* life. Any amount of observer work required is worth regaining your voice. Quite possibly, there is a point of impact where the system of your mouth was shut down within your brain. Observing the moment you became silent is half the battle. The next half involves you observing that impact from the present, not from the past. The past is where you lost your power. The present is where you gain clarity and are able to change the meaning of the damage done at the point of impact in order to heal. Does that make sense? It is so exciting to imagine that you are so close to the breakthrough that will plant your feet in your next-level life!

Ancient script in the chapter of Ezekiel features a cool story in the valley of the dry bones that should resonate with all of you who have lost your voice. God is asking Ezekiel in this bone graveyard if these bones can live. It seems that Ezekiel should be asking God if the bones can come to life, right? But God tells Ezekiel to speak life into these bones. As Ezekiel speaks, the dry bones fully come to life. God could have easily demonstrated the same thing, but he instead gave the power to speak to Ezekiel. A similar thing happens in the Book of Matthew when God says that if you speak to your mountain with even an ounce of faith, your mountain can be moved. *Your* mountains move to the sound of *your* voice!

Your mountain, your voice, your victory!

188 • AMY WESTBROOK

It is in the showing up and speaking up that hunger starts to resemble a steamroller! The discipline of incorporating this into our fight to mobility and maximum freedom inspires us to grow up.

ᏟROW UP

FALSE COPING

There is a lot of growing up that goes on as one battles for freedom. Freedom to walk, freedom to achieve, freedom to be. Where you find a next-level life, you find a renewed level of maturity.

Honestly, I had to grow up in my emotions and in my lifestyle choices in order to create the ultimate environment in which to heal. If I wanted to defy the odds forecasted for my future, I had to grow up. Most steps I had to implement were simplistic in nature, but they took discipline, which always involves maturity.

My sleep pattern had to be micro-managed because carrying my body during the day was so taxing. That was not always fun when the party or plans had just gotten started, yet I needed my sleep. My eating habits had to become superior to what they already were in order to bathe my cells in nutrition and to avoid the internal damage that a lot of new medications could eventually create. My thoughts had to become a machine of positivity in order to be capable of continued physical therapy with exorbitant amounts of pain and lackluster results on many days. I was accustomed to a lifetime of applying my body to physical rigor with excellent results.

One of the things I frequently do on my podcast, L!ve with Amy, is address a subject no one wants to talk about, but one nearly every person experiences. Transparent talk transforms. I have seen it perform miracles through ministry and establish firm foundations in both life and business. So, here we go.

False coping mechanisms keep us paralyzed. As I script this, I think back to thirty years ago and my battle with an intense addiction to nicotine. The lie in that coping mechanism was that it was helping me manage my anxiety and chaos, when in reality it was creating another crisis that I would have to overcome. It was, as such, a false coping mechanism.

My friends could smoke for a week or a month and then lay those cigarettes down and not think about them for an extended amount of time. Not me. Once I started smoking, I had an insatiable appetite for nicotine, and it was actually playing right into my anxiety struggles. There is not space enough in this book to address all of our false coping mechanisms that lead us to needing more coping mechanisms—or at the very least another demon to overcome. It's a big enough topic for an entirely separate book.

Stay with me if you are an "all in" for next-level living. Removing false coping mechanisms is initially frightening, but in the end, it allows you to uncover and overcome the root cause of your need for that mechanism. This is where the rubber meets the road. Stop and look honestly and maturely at the coping mechanisms that you have justified as "helpful." Label them for what they really are in your life, perhaps just another thing you have to feel guilty, shameful, or stressed about removing from your life.

I'm talking straight-up about alcohol, drugs, men, women, food, shopping, gossip, workaholism, and social media obsession. You have read to this point either because you need out of the "wheelchair" life has placed you in, or you are longing for your next-level life (or both). This subject must be breeched candidly if you want real results. If you *truly* are not messing around, this subject must be of serious contemplation. We each must be willing to grow up!

With every step of freedom I gained out of darkness from my past and the destructive behaviors of my past, I most certainly reached a new level of maturity that had to be embraced. The definition of embrace is "to hold closely in one's arms, especially as a sign of affection, or to accept or support a belief, theory, or change willingly and enthusiastically." Here is a helpful tip: to embrace doesn't mean it has to feel good in the beginning. To embrace means you have agreed and *aligned* to head purposefully in a new direction. The concept must be present in order for successful results to result from this newfound maturity.

Maturity calls for discipline, which is why we have so many immature adults walking around. Very few people want to do the work even though it produces gold. And, in all fairness, very few people even know what the work is. They are raising kids, running companies, leading teams, and making a mess of their personal relationships. Immaturity places children at a huge disadvantage, sent out into the world desperately needing the ability to make grounded decisions and maintain mental strength. If you have immature kids and teenagers, look in the mirror. Maturity on your part can help solve that challenge.

Maturity *always* calls for a level of "self" to be set aside. When you find a person heavily focused on self, you find a lot of immaturity. Maturity addresses age-old belief systems that are wreaking havoc on the people we engage with, and it unleashes true, lasting success. At first, we start kicking and screaming like a three-year-old, pouting, lower lip out, arms flailing. Realistically, this may not be what you do as an adult, but it often looks that way when observed in others. Immaturity craves things that keep you paralyzed. And, oh Lord, I thought I was so mature in my own immaturity!

I was satisfying my cravings of all the world had to offer in an effort to feel free. The result of all that was chains. As we align our maturity with our actions, a power we have never known begins to move us, not from point A to point B but from point B to point D then from point D to point G.

Paul addresses the immaturity of the leaders of the church in Corinthians. In 1 Corinthians 3, he said, "Brothers and sisters, I could not address you as people who live by the Spirit but as people who are still worldly—mere infants in Christ. I gave you milk, not solid food, for you were not yet ready for it. Indeed, you are still not ready. You are still worldly." Sometimes we want the solid food, but we are only capable of taking in mere milk. The immaturity of these leaders was clearly keeping them from their next-level life.

Speak up, show up, grow up. This is an act of your will, not a feeling—at least, not at first. But I can confirm that when the feeling sets in, it holds so much substance and grounding that you will feel powerful and proud. *You will begin to know that you are in control and are no longer being controlled.* The desire and craving for what is paralyzing you will begin to grow dim. It will feel like it's at an arm's distance instead of within you. Maturity, growing up, begins with owning what is yours and taking action. Immaturity and "self" lie to us about what maturity will do for us in your lives. Exchanging pleasure for pain in order to eventually gain freedom requires maturity.

This idea of growing up and out of paralysis leads me to share with you a shocking fact about my youth: I showed pigs.

My father was an agriculture professor, so we did not have a choice. We were enrolled in 4-H and had to pick an animal. Because I'm smart, I chose pigs. As you show pigs in the ring, you guide them around with a small leather bat versus holding onto them as you have to with some of the other animals. Plus, the babies were beyond adorable.

My job, year after year, was to tend to my pigs: groom them, wash them, brush them, and make them beautiful—you know, clean all the mud and gunk off of them just for them to run straight back to their wallowing hole. You and I do the same things if maturity and resolvolution do not take their course. We wallow within our stuck-ness. We also get all cleaned up only to head right back to the mud. Pigs wallow, not people! There is a time under the sun for everything, and that includes a day of reckoning for maturity. Wallowing leads to certain paralysis. A commitment to maturity leads to a willingness to discover the reason you wallow, and then the courage to walk out of it.

There is power in responsibility. It grounds us and tends to get our attention in order for us to grow up and out of our roadblocks. We are responsible for our showing up, speaking up, and growing up. Maturity perseveres, maturity forgives. Maturity is not offended. Maturity consults. Maturity responds versus reacts. Maturity feels really, really good. Maturity takes ownership of one's circumstances. Mature eyes are not hyper-focused on everyone else. Maturity is not always mad. Maturity chooses positive action. Maturity embraces discipline. Maturity knows when to stop talking.

I have been walking a journey of maturity with a friend of mine—a journey that millions of women are also walking, or at least wildly desiring to walk. There are so many people struggling in silence with this same false coping mechanism with which she suffered. She found a way out, and it took a major move of maturity, large doses of Jesus and resolvolution on her part. She had been a "Mommy's sippy cup" wine girl her entire life. Her life was in control, out of control, in control, out of control. She purposed herself to stop time and time again, to no avail. The dilemma seemed to be, even if subconsciously, "I know I'm more than a social drinker, but I'm not a full-blown alcoholic needing AA, so I'll keep going regardless of how defeated I'm feeling."

She discovered an online group called Sober Sis. The founder of this group spoke straight to her heart about the problem she and millions of others share: gray area drinking. She wasn't an alcoholic, but she also wasn't able to quit. Gray area drinking had finally come to a head for my friend. She maturely (still with fear and a little hesitation) got involved with the program and joined a Sober Sis online group. This group was full of successful, high-achieving women who know they have a problem and aren't sure what to call it. A lot of women feel like a fish out of water as they determine to get alcohol out of their life once and for all. Gray area drinkers have few areas to go to seek help other than counseling.

Sober Sis also addresses the reality that women don't fit in because all her "circles" are drinking circles. Engaging with those circles entices you to give in to avoid having everyone else shame you about your next-level life decision to stop drinking. That is a real pain I've suffered on again and off again for twenty years, and it feels lonely! It's hard to see your nearest and dearest friends at an event in which you weren't included because you aren't a big drinker. It can make you feel less than over a decision you made that is best for you. My friend experiences this repeatedly. But the further along she goes, the more resolute she becomes in her decision and in helping other women maturely come out of the paralysis they feel from "wine-itis."

I am reminded of the couple of years my husband and I were teaching healthy living classes in our home. Our class members were people serious about their next-level life when it came to health. They were *not* messing around. Out of maturity, they were taking responsibility for their lack of self-care. As we began to address something similar to false coping mechanisms with unhealthy living, we learned that "craving" meant "control." Each person created their own intervention statement or intervention action (preparation) so that when faced with a temptation that could throw them off course, they were ready to intervene and protect themselves.

One of those intervention statements was, "No thanks, I am not craving that right now." But we all knew we were actually recalibrating our brain saying, "No thanks, I am not controlled by that temptation." Interrupting your brain's default patterns is paramount to designing your life with consciously chosen thought patterns. *Maturity puts a hard stop on default living, which closes the gap on the life you live versus the life you desire.* There is no better way to accelerate your income than to invest in your brain!

THOSE DOUBLE DOORS

As we transition through this journey called life with its unexpected outcomes, there can be an awkward type of sadness and loss at each transition point, even as you gain the beautiful future. I recall the day my outpatient therapist, Sharyn, discussed that it was time to fly, meaning leave outpatient therapy at the hospital and begin solo training protocol, possibly with a trainer.

In the middle of our therapy session, as we talked about what that would look like, my tears caught me off guard. I rolled over onto the exercise mat in an effort to hide those tears until I figured out what they meant. After I returned home that day, I journaled out those racing thoughts. "Last day, this place, but I have lived here so long. My refuge, my lifeline. But I am not healed yet! How do I leave? How do I say goodbye? It is not finished. I am so sad, yet I should be so happy? There is a feeling of sadness, loss, incompleteness. Yet gratefulness is rising up from the depth of my being for all that has been accomplished here in this place."

That afternoon I went out and got my therapist Sharyn a card. In it, I wrote "Thank you for being so hopeful for and focused on my recovery. What a journey, and I am glad I spent it with you. You will forever be a part of my life." I also got a small plaque that read "When I count my blessings I count you twice."

The day came to transition. We said our goodbyes, and I gave her the card and gift. As I faced those double doors of the rehab hospital that I had passed through so many times before, I wondered, "Do I just walk out?" And that's exactly what I did. I walked out using my cane, and I drove myself home. The hospital simply did not best serve me any longer. Are you dependent on something that no longer best serves you? We all do that. We attach ourselves to things that no longer serve our purposes and goals. Also, not all departures are bad. With new perspective, we can view them as steppingstones. I went from the wheelchair to the walker, from the walker to the cane, from the cane to the freedom of walking without a cane in order to reach my ultimate goal of running.

That Easter morning, sitting in that room with my head cheerleader in her blue polka-dotted dress, I knew I would someday run. That cane leaning against the bathroom vanity was not serving me well any longer. Steppingstones. Transitions. Showing up, speaking up, and growing up produced 1,100 sessions of physical therapy that have led to transition after transition.

THE AFTER PARTY

I t wasn't really home, but it was. A year and a half prior to my surgery, we had moved into a temporarily leased house. We sold our first home to start our custom home building company and had been working to build a new custom home designed just for us. The new home was in South Austin, where we could hopefully hit the refresh button and create a life I falsely believed would erase the spiritual pain I held inside—the pain of lost dreams, lost faith, and lost mobility.

The new home was scheduled to be complete just a few weeks later. Now reconciled spiritually and needing the love and support of our inner circle because of my physical situation, that brand new, almost completed home didn't make as much sense any longer. There was already great debate about where and how I would come home. Both the current leased home and the house we were building had upstairs bedrooms. The doctors had counseled us that stairs were not in my immediate future, if ever. They would not release me into a home with stairs. So, an additional newly leased one-story home awaited our arrival.

I did not expect the reaction I had when we arrived home. As Greg pushed my wheelchair through the front door, a flood of images ran through my mind, images of who I was the last time I had been in this house. Those images included running in the neighborhood and power-pushing a stroller to the neighborhood pool and back. They included loads of activities! I was overwhelmed with emotion related to what was. I sat in the living room and cried over the images that reflected my past jubilation, motion, and the joy of being mobile. I cried over the images that reflected my ability to move about and do things for my daughter and my husband. I had to pull it together, though, because it was time for Playdough with my daughter.

We had just a couple of nights left until we would move into the new home. A hospital bed awaited me and had been placed downstairs in the family room. Next to the bed was my portable toilet because the doorway to the downstairs powder bath was not wide enough for my wheelchair to pass through. There were boxes stacked throughout the house that had been packed by strangers. Why on earth I did not stay in the hospital one more week until the house was moved, I will never know. The new movement, new schedule, and new surroundings threw my body into a new dimension of pain. I had spasms like I had never experienced. My rib cage and core felt like they were being crushed.

Nighttime brought an entirely new set of issues. Lauren insisted on sleeping by me in the twin-size hospital bed made of hard plastic. Once I got home, I could barely pull her off of me. I begged Greg to sleep downstairs to reassure me that he could help me if I needed him. He brought Lauren's twin mattress from upstairs and chucked it in the corner. Here we were, camping out in our family room, boxes piled all around us, with a porta potty in the corner to boot! These were miserable conditions, really!

My family showed up to pack the last items in the kitchen, and my girlfriends graciously arrived the next night to pack my closet and undergarment drawers. Look, some things just cannot be left to strange men to pack and move! Does a man know how to pack jewelry, makeup, or shoes? No. But the girls did. My out-patient therapy would begin in the hospital facility the next week, and before then, there was a lot of adjusting and a lot of unpacking to do, and one of those was an activity I could not do.

NEW HOUSE

As unnerving as it was to have people packing my belongings, I was overwhelmed with gratefulness. A For Sale sign was going up at the home we had built for ourselves. Unexpected outcomes call for us to adjust, adjust, adjust. By the grace of God, the church offered their moving ministry. Fifteen men showed up bright and early Saturday morning and moved our entire house from one place to the other. They were finished by 1pm. I wasn't there. I had been taken to my sister's just down the highway. What you don't know won't make you crazy! I was in no shape to be present. I just prayed they got it all in a semi-correct place. Then again, it didn't matter much anyway. Reality was coming at me fast.

Greg picked me up from my sister's house to take me to the new house. I had been miserable most of the day because we just could not get my pain under control. As we drew closer to the new address, I internally began to weep and ache. I didn't have a "home" to come to, nor a car, as Greg had turned in my leased vehicle while I was in the hospital. I was in a wheelchair, dependent on others to transfer me, cook for me, and transport me. I could not even take a shower unless Greg was there with me to help me get me in and out. I have never felt so out of place in life. The vulnerability created from that wheelchair life was of great magnitude.

Where was the warmth of my life? I wanted my old house back, the one before the leased houses. The home my baby was born in. I needed my mom! "Oh God," I cried out! How was I going to do this? At least I could have come home to my car sitting in the driveway...something familiar...but that too was gone.

Greg parked us in the driveway, and I told him I needed a minute to get myself together. In that moment, the hollow feeling was immeasurable, yet I felt cared for, yet alone, yet grateful. I was a bit of a mess. The sight of one of my dearest friends pulled me out of this pit as she greeted us from the front door. She always showed up at just the right minute! As we came through the door, she was going on and on about what a great house we were moving into. It took my mind and heart off of the internal ache.

The layout of the house was perfect for my wheelchair, and the shower accommodated my shower chair. There was space enough for Greg to transfer me and lift me out safely. There was plenty of space for the bedside toilet. My setup was such that I could push to standing on the walker and then just pivot to the toilet seat. It worked for a long while.

Once the move was over and everyone had gone home, I finally began to grieve what had transpired over the past two months. I was grieving something that had already past: the hospital stay; the feelings of being alone, missing Lauren and Greg; the way I lay there for two months in that sterile environment, frustrated with the disgusting things I had to deal with; depending on others for basic daily function. Now in this safe environment, I let go. Alone at home in my bed, I could process through all of it. I sobbed and ached in the silence of this new place until my wails drowned out the silence.

The next day, with the grieving session behind me, it was time to heal, and I was not messing around! This was a birth, not a death.

I continued to challenge myself physically as the weeks passed. I also continued to feed myself spiritually. Sitting on the sofa one day, it dawned on me that I should read the story in the Bible about Jesus healing the paralytic. And there it was: the part of the story I had never paid attention to. It washed over me like a flood. The story of the paralytic is about a physical healing, but it is also about a spiritual healing. Just before Jesus instructed the paralytic to take his mat and walk home, he discussed the importance of his spiritual healing. Point being, the priority to heal His spirit was way more important to Jesus than the priority to heal His physical nature. Sitting there wrapped in grace, I realized He had healed me spiritually. By His words, spoken in those dark hours to the miraculous timing of the surgery to the closing of my cord in front of the surgeon's eyes, all to remind me that He was and is and is to come. He is who He says He is. He had been all I had in those dark moments, and He created situations where the intimacy of our relationship had gone where few men go.

He did not desert me, leave me, or forsake me. As I knocked during those desperate days leading up to surgery, He came in like a flood. His voice came, His church came, His healing came. His timing was within the thickness of a piece of paper. The dream that was completely lost had been rekindled: to speak, write, and teach. He had restored my gift of faith that had, at one time, been able to move mountains. From battered and broken faith to a faith that could inspire a nation. A kind of soul work happened in that hospital that is difficult to attach to human words. No longer was I spiritually paralyzed.

REFLECTION

I t was a Thursday morning, and the hospital was in full swing. Exactly eighteen months had passed since Lauren and Greg came to move me out of room 217 and I'd come for an appointment with my rehab doctor. Being back there was overwhelming. Recalling the day the ambulance rolled me through those front double doors, there was so much uncertainty. How foreign this place looked upon arrival, yet how familiar a home it was on the day I left. Returning on this day, I will never forget the smell. The pungent, constant hospital smell. As I observed the hustle and bustle, I recall lying in my hospital bed, thinking how oblivious the outside world is to the world inside a hospital day-in and day-out. The pain, the heroes, the fear, and the miracles. From my first-hand experience, I honor and praise you if you are a healthcare professional. The vulnerability of the patients for whom you so artfully and skillfully care is something quite amazing. Thank you, from all of us who have ever needed you. Never downplay the impact of your showing up for work each day.

What a dichotomy as I sat there watching the decadent ceremony for Michael Jackson, as the world stood to its feet to cheer the "Greatest Entertainer in the World." Here, in this place, a man passed by in a wheelchair with a prosthetic leg, one scooted his own wheelchair, and yet another entered the café as a quadriplegic in a high-headrest electric chair. I pondered reality versus fantasy, and tears rolled down my cheeks as I made notes in my journal. I really hoped the people in the cafeteria didn't think I was crying over Michael Jackson!

There was a man there who obviously had suffered a stroke, and a man, possibly his son, was there to assist him. He was lifted from his chair with an awkward transfer into his vehicle. Hope. They all needed hope. They didn't see the beginning; they cannot see the end. My heart broke for their situation, their battle. My new roots of compassion are deep and unending for trauma and its fallout. Thank God the therapist and doctors approached us all with a vision of hope.

There were people there who carry others. They carry them with their words and their smiles, and they carry them by returning each day to care for them. The young man who transferred me to Brackenridge hospital for several urgent procedures passed by the door. In walked Deborah, my favorite nurse who had walked with me through so much, including through the "not-cathing project!"

"Amy! You are walking. When did you start walking? This is so wonderful!" I then saw Lynn from a distance. She was such a good nurse. Really thorough, informative, and involved, all qualities you appreciate in the midst of a foreign storm, the kind of support you need in the desert.

I headed for the second floor just to pay a visit. As I rounded the corner, there she was, my first physical therapist, Ellen. She and Cynthia were the ones there the day I took that first step. Ellen probably was the closest thing to a mom that I encountered while in the hospital. Ellen and I had a conversation out in the hallway. She reflected on "what a scary time it was." She said, "I just remember you lying there, not able to move. We simply didn't know what was going to happen."

Before I left, I had to go to the fourth floor to look at the ambulatory machine, the machine that mimics walking. I looked through the glass door and there it was, but I had forgotten about the mirror directly in front of the tread belt. My reflection in that mirror was now a very different portrait. No wheelchair, no walker, no pajamas. Upright, mobile, grateful! As imperfect as my gait still remains and as pronounced as my nerve pain is, I am grateful. I was flooded with emotion as I sat down and journaled all I was taking in.

IT IS A RE-RE WORLD

The worst feeling in the world is the feeling that you are being left behind. It hurts when others are moving forward, and we are working our butt off yet still stuck. A wave of that feeling would hit me off-guard on the days I could glance up and see the runners in my neighborhood passing by. It's a feeling that can become a source of anxiety and disappointment in ourselves. The Freedom Success Method™ was birthed to resolve that feeling in as many lives as possible.

After a few years being home, I recall the day I found myself once again on the couch. There on the sofa, I remember watching Kelly Ripa do her thing on Live with Kelly and Michael. She was living her best life at the height of her career, while I was like a fish outside of its aquarium. All of my friends were building their families and their careers, just like I once was. Everyone was engaged in their success, and there I was, still in this mess, trying to walk in a straight line. The more I thought about it, the deeper I sank into the sofa. I finally hit a threshold inside of me, that threshold we ALL have inside that finally says, "Enough!" That was it. I made a soul decision to move.

The first thing I had to do was build new habits, and none of them involved the sofa or TV. The irony of this is that I honestly hate TV. For years, I would have been perfectly fine with no TV. But as time ebbed and flowed, I would sit down in front of the TV and begin to go into a feeling-less trance. Subconsciously, it was moving me out of my circumstances and into nothingness. There were moments when I felt so unusable and irrelevant in my desert existence. Does this sound familiar? Are you entertaining activities and habits in your life that you actually abhor or that do not line up with your core values? Have these "hated" activities numbed your existence, but in turn...let's say it together...kept you paralyzed? Your next level-life is all about your new habits.

The new habits I implemented allowed me to form the non-profit organization that I had dreamed of for many years. Those habits led me to negotiate and design a primetime morning radio show that has continued on and off for twelve years and morphed into my podcast, L!ve with Amy.

Here is the truth about you, my friend: circumstances do not define who you are; they refine who you are becoming! There is an anthem that recording artist Pitbull released titled "I Believe That We Win!" in response to the pandemic opposition the world has faced. The lyrics are about rising higher than we were where we left off. Let it be your anthem, starting today!

Life is still moving. That is true. But, let it be known that in our darkness, as unexpected outcomes rock our worlds, we actually become more qualified, wiser, and more promotable than those who seem to be passing us by through hard-sell and dog-eat-dog tactics. I lived that life for thirty-five years in sales and marketing. I've seen people in my community hard-sell themselves to the top, and it's a bit cringy to watch. I've also seen several of them fall from the unsustainability of it all.

But, one who rises out of the mire? That is a person I can grow and gain from. That is a person worth following and listening to. I want that person on my team, for they know what it is like to foster hunger and scale a mountain! They know how to do hard things and make hard decisions. Leaders, managers, and owners, serve yourself well by looking for the stories behind the people you work with.

Unexpected outcomes. We often don't see them coming. Some we can anticipate from a slow drip of circumstances, while others completely blindside us. My estimated two-hour surgery and three days in the hospital turned into a five-and-a-half-hour surgery and two months in the hospital—and then into the rest of my life. The next twelve years of my life produced other radical unexpected outcomes. I didn't see infidelity coming in my eighteen-year marriage. The pain experienced from losing our family unit was immense. I also did not see, years later, that I was building my new life after divorce on a pile of deceit and smoke and mirrors. The ending of one relationship caused utter loss and grief. The experience of the other caused complete shock and a level of disbelief that required trauma therapy to rise out of it.

This was right about the time in my story when I accepted the title Queen of Unexpected Outcomes. It was not a title I chose; it chose me.

But all is never lost. In the depths of my marriage ending, that voice of wisdom visited me yet again. That voice that I am so accustomed to hearing the second I need it. What I heard proved itself true for the next many years.

I woke up on a Saturday morning, sat up in bed, and heard thoughts that were not my own say, "I have made a way for you in the desert." Past tense. "I have made a way for you in the desert." Wisdom from on high. My husband and I were separated, and I had just gone back to a sales and marketing job at a radio station. I could do it like the back of my hand, and it made sense in the middle of chaos not to try and reinvent myself at that moment. Within a few short months, I earned top sales executive status, built a strong client base, and was rewarded with bonuses. I "have" made a way.

This was an incredible relief, giving me the wherewithal to heal and to help Lauren heal. Lauren was struggling so severely that it hurt every cell in my body. One day, I was sitting with her on the bedroom floor trying to help her ten-year-old self comprehend that she would, and we would be okay. The resources I had been building for years led me to one of the best therapists on the planet, and he guided Lauren back to life alongside the Holy Spirit. My daughter's strong mental health is also credited to her strong faith and knowing without a doubt that she is cared for by an all-encompassing God. The resources you need will show up exactly when you need them. Lean in hard to Christ and hone eyes that can truly see and ears that can truly hear.

Time passed and my career soared, I purchased my very own home, and I hit a milestone birthday. This life! The greatest joys and accomplishments birthed in the middle of trauma. Each time, I had a belief that it was the last unexpected outcome and that "crisis freedom" was on the way.

Unexpected outcomes birth what I call a "re-re" life for all of us. From that point forward, our lives become a project and movement of reset, restart, reinvent, repair, regenerate, reform, or reboot. Some days are a hard pill to swallow, and we do not have to love those days. Regardless, the truth remains: Either stay immobile for the rest of our life or live in the present realm, shifting your being to the fact it is now a "re-re" world. Embrace it, and birth your next-level life. The act of embracing will break the chains of lockdown.

Many times, reset and realign are not actions that have to be brooded over and assessed to death. Many times, it just takes awareness. In a moment, a split second, the revelation is laid bare and suddenly, hallelujah, you can process, redirect, or reject. Even now in a "re-re" state of mind, we take on the power stance of positive pursuit, releasing your mind of what was and liberating it to the precious present in order to accomplish your life mission.

A life has ensued that is miraculous and mysterious. My stability and ability to thrive in some form or another is to the credit of a God who promises to never leave us or forsake us, and to all I gained during my journey out of physical paralysis. A life that is, on one hand, still imperfect physically and on the other, flourishing, loving, and full of life. This can happen. We don't have to live in the depths of despair while a crisis plays out in our lives. Because every truth and process I have shared contributes to success and peace in the midst of our unexpected outcomes.

Life ebbs and flows. Unexpected outcomes are a part of life. They will always work themselves out. You will make it; this too shall pass. But we absolutely have to do the work set before us. I'm writing this chapter early in the morning, and as I sit here in this quiet space, my spirit can testify it is extraordinarily full of peace, sound mind, intact emotions. My professional life is more sound than ever before. I have a knowing that God is with me, even though I am in the midst of a storm of deceit and uncertainty. I do not hang onto what I don't know or cannot see. I live in this moment *because* the rest I cannot see.

The love and relationship I have with my daughter has lifted me out of hell more than once. Countless days, I can recall seeing her face, her curls, experiencing her presence, and observing as she brought me back from nothingness. Regardless of all that you have just read about, Lauren and I believe that we have lived a life together full of fun and truly precious moments. We have scaled walls we never dreamed possible. We have seen each other at our lowest as well as at very high peaks. We have seen our girl power at work over and over together. The gratefulness I feel for that child being in my life is indescribable. She is gracious, she is giving, she is compassionate, she is fun and thoughtful. She has loved me, she has comforted me, she has physically assisted me, and she has been respectful of the fact that I am her best friend but also her God-appointed authority. As you can see, the act of being a mom to Lauren is without a doubt the greatest joy of my existence. What a liar the devil was to tell me anything counter to that all those years prior to motherhood. Now I am gifted with her wisdom, as she becomes an amazing young woman.

There are people in my life who have alluded to this relationship as odd because of the level of connection we have built. The way she and I see it is that we are the luckiest mom and daughter on the planet to have each other. And, yes, we have an extraordinary bond because we have survived, arm in arm, extraordinary circumstances and come out thriving every time! Never mind the truth that Lauren once actually said, "Mom, I honestly feel like someone is about to emerge from behind our walls and say 'Cut! that's a wrap!'"

In this moment, there is love and *purposeful* passion for what I am called to do in life. My passion and preparedness to encourage and lift people out of paralysis and lockdown has never been stronger. My end goal is to motivate the planet into positive action as they rise from unexpected outcomes and into a next-level existence. I am not just a survivor; I am a thriver! There is a way for you. Darkness is not your destiny, nor is it mine. Does it take work? Yes! Is your freedom worth fighting for? Yes!

As I was attempting to walk in the rehab hospital, the voice of wisdom told me, "You are stronger than you think! Stand up. Stand up and walk." And you, my friend, are stronger than you think you are. You have never exhausted your resources because you are resourceful. You are never alone because He sees you. Rarely will anyone other than our maker understand the depths to which unexpected outcomes can take us. He knows you. He understands your pain and frustration! In the words of recording artist Lauren Daigle, "Look up, child!"

Are you anywhere near where I was in the midst of feeling stuck? Do you know that your next-level life is waiting for you? Do you need a guide to help you cross the finish line? It would be my honor to walk you through The Freedom Success Method™. It will merge with your unique personal story and bring radical mobility. Nothing pumps up my core more than supporting people as they implement the method and see results within their own story.

Remember, if you want maximum freedom, you must be willing to submit yourself to the surgical table. Many times, doing so is our only hope. It begins with a decision and then a declaration to all those committed to the success of your journey. Next, the dedication to finish strong—dedicating yourself no matter the cost without knowing the future. These three actions are the catalyst to showing up, speaking up, and growing up. In your journey, know without a doubt there is always a hope and a future. Humility breeds power and progression. Hunger that sustains momentum will become fierce as you take steps out of an act of will.

The sidebars of life contribute to the sum of the parts of each person. I hang on to John 16:32 when dealing with side-bars: "In this world you will have trouble but take heart I have overcome the world!" signed in red by Jesus. Amen! Do not go through life without cheerleaders. And finally, *my friend, as you heed the voice of wisdom, you can walk out of the "wheelchair" life has placed you in.*

Now, let me answer the questions on everyone's mind. Am I running yet and am I walking in those high heel red shoes? The answer is no…but yes. I still engage in physical training every week, and have not run …YET! But I am running the race set before me, and I will run it to win. As for those high heel shoes? Not yet, but I AM walking in "high-*healed* shoes."

ABOUT THE AUTHOR

Amy Westbrook is an entrepreneur, former paraplegic, former radio show host, podcaster, and the founder of Souled Out ministries. She spent thirty-five years as a sales and marketing executive, specializing in both the hospitality and media industries, and is the mastermind behind The Freedom Success Method™, an online course designed to guide students to their next-level life. Westbrook has used her infectious passion to speak to audiences about the fact that they can live their dream life—despite life's unexpected setbacks.

Amy currently resides in Austin, Texas.

www.LiveWithAmy.com

Instagram: @LiveWithAmy.w

ACKNOWLEDGEMENTS

With enormous appreciation and heartfelt sincerity, thank you...

To the doctors, countless nurses, and technicians at Seton Hospital and Health South Rehabilitation Hospital who tirelessly cared for me, kept my dignity intact and spirits high, and never gave up on me.

To the countless physical therapists who have believed for me and in me, and who also never gave up on me, including Jeff Gotte and his team at Practical Fitness; Molly at LifeTime Fitness; Garrett Salpeter, Steve Haldeman, and the team at Neufit; Michele Harris at CHARM (Center for Healing and Regenerative Medicine); and Nanci Patch at Moksha Pilates. You have been a priceless piece of the fabric in my experience of conquering the unconquerable! We have "achieved," and for that I am forever grateful. I also honor the countless other professionals who have served and loved me! You know who you are, and how much I love and appreciate you.

To Dr. Womack, thank you for caring for me like only you can, and for your ever-evolving expertise that I am the beneficiary of year-in and year-out.

To Dr. Kemper, thank you for your humanness and for the brilliance you executed in the OR to keep me on my feet.

To Dr. Arizmendez, thank you for your rehabilitation assistance, starting from ground zero!

To my other many specialist, including Dr. Melody Denson, Dr. Craig Kuhns, and Dr. David Harris, thank you!

To Lauren, I acknowledge all that you have gone through in the many phases of my recovery. You did not deserve to walk this struggle with me, but you have chosen to let it make you a better young woman. You are the joy and light of my life, always!

To my immediate family, thank you for embracing the new me and for all the concessions you continually make to ensure I am accommodated.

To my precious friends who, year after year after year, have cheered me on and supported all of my trials. Thank you for accommodating me. Your compassion has been the wind beneath my wings. Not a single ounce of anything any of you has done for me has gone unnoticed. I have been and continue to be acutely aware, always humbled and grateful, through and through.

www.ingramcontent.com/pod-product-compliance
Lightning Source LLC
LaVergne TN
LVHW051509080426
835509LV00017B/1990